Love Is the Answer

Samantha Lee is a woman of many parts. She not only acts, sings, lectures and broadcasts, but she also writes novels. She has long been an active enthusiast in the field of health and fitness, and is the author of *Fit to Be Fifty* and *All By Myself*. She lives in London with her son.

Also by Samantha Lee

Fit to Be Fifty
All By Myself

Love
is the
answer-
now what
was the question

?

Samantha Lee

VISTA

First published in Great Britain 1998
as a Vista paperback original

Vista is an imprint of the Cassell Group
Wellington House, 125 Strand, London WC2R 0BB

A catalogue record for this book is available
from the British Library.

ISBN 0 575 60246 5

Designed and typeset by
Fishtail Design

Printed and bound in Great Britain
by Cox & Wyman Ltd, Reading, Berks

99 98   10 9 8 7 6 5 4 3 2 1

To Jack and Charlie – with love and thanks

Contents

LOVE FOR OTHERS

LOVE FOR LIFE

Prologue

'What is this thing called love?'

Love is that elusive something which everyone wants, regardless of age, sex, socio-economic group, race, creed or colour. It means many things to many people. Lover's embrace or grandchild's hug. Praise from a respected tutor or the wagging of a grateful dog's tail. Sophisticates sneer at it. Lonely souls pretend to despise it. But the truth is that we all need love to survive. Without it we wither and die like a flower deprived of water and sunlight.

Love is the most powerful force in the universe. And it is irresistible. It benefits both the giver and the receiver in equal measure.

So how, if you feel you are not receiving your fair share, do you get more of this priceless commodity?

Simple.

You give more out. Giving love freely and unconditionally opens up the love channels and lets more love in. Grabbing, demanding or abusing love cuts off the flow, closes down the supply.

In the late twentieth century love and sex seem to have become synonymous. They are no such thing – though they may be complementary. Movies and pop songs pound out sentimentality rather than true sentiment. Luurv. The emotional equivalent of muzak. Soulless, shallow sex and its darker cousin, pornography, aim their darts at a populace hungry for the quick fix. And like the quick fix, they leave the user empty, unsatisfied, demanding more.

Hollywood used to paint on a much broader canvas, giving us love as justice (*Mr Deeds Goes to Washington*), devotion (*Mrs Miniver*) and self-sacrifice (*Casablanca*). Love was equated with high ideals. And people rose to the occasion.

Today's one-dimensional, cinematic concept of love as obligatory bonk, twenty minutes into the action, has greatly devalued the currency. Love is more than slickly packaged sensuality acted out on the big screen to afford the viewer a cheap, voyeuristic thrill. Yet given our escalating fascination with computers and the lack of human interaction in many modern lives, these images may be the only yardstick by which the next generation can judge what love is supposed to be about. It is vital that we teach our children, and ourselves, the value of loving wisely and well. Without love we are in danger of obliterating the entire human race.

Love is an all-encompassing notion which, if everyone practised it daily, would eliminate wars at a stroke and allow humanity to realize its vast potential for good. Famine could become a thing of a less civilized past. For if swords were beaten into ploughshares and the money spent on armaments was diverted into the production of wheat rather than weapons, there would be more than enough to feed all the nations of the earth.

A high ideal? An impossible dream?

Not if we all took individual responsibility. Not if we stopped passing the buck. Not if we didn't expect somebody else to start the ball rolling. The way to make the dream come true is to begin with ourselves. Now. Today.

As Confucius said, 'The longest journey begins with the first step.'

Love is power. A power for good. It's all around. And it's free. You don't have to invest cash in it. Just faith and energy and trust. It's there, waiting to be extracted – like ore from a gold mine. We all have a bottomless well of the stuff inside us begging to be used.

So why are so many of us dying of thirst?

Mostly because we have such a narrow definition of this precious commodity. Nowadays the view seems to be that if you're not in 'a permanent relationship' you are doomed to live a loveless existence. Nothing could be further from the truth. Love is much bigger than 'you and me against the world'. Love *is* the world. Look at Mother Teresa. Do you think her life lacked love?

In essence love has three faces which roughly correspond to the trinity of body, mind and spirit. Each element complements the other two. They are interactive and indivisible. They are . . .

Sexual connection

Bodily passion, carnal knowledge, physical ecstasy, mutual satisfaction, the engine of procreation, call it what you will, good old-fashioned sex is built into our genetic programming. It was invented to ensure the survival of the species. At its best it is pure unadulterated pleasure and more fun than a wagonload of monkeys. But it is only part of the equation and, to be honest, the most ephemeral and fleeting part.

Nurturing

Less basic, arising from the mind rather than the body, nurturing is the selfless face of love which gives with no thought of return. Paradoxically, we get a colossal return in the pure joy of seeing the beloved (whether person, pet or plant) blossom and grow under our care. Nurturing, of self and others, spreads loving out from the closed shop of coupledom to the wider horizon of family and friends. It encourages a stable, mutual support system which enables the intellectual part of the organism to thrive and to experiment from a position of safety.

Compassion

This is the spiritual dimension of love that binds us to each other, to the planet and to our own personal maker, whether we conceive that to be an old man with a white beard, Mother Earth, the pantheistic Great Spirit of the native American or the metaphysical face of eternity. At rock bottom we are all atoms whirling in space. We were fashioned to co-operate with, not to obliterate each other. A compassionate viewpoint is an altogether more esoteric ideal that either sexual love or nurturing. There may be no immediate, obvious payback, only the long-term goal of making the world a better place for everyone, including ourselves, to live in. Because of this it is perhaps the hardest aspect of love to put into practice. In the long run it may also be the most important for our survival. Compassion is loving for its own sake. It involves making a contribution, leading by example, considering the other person's point of view and, as its ultimate expression, being prepared for self-sacrifice. It brings with it wider understanding, personal awareness and inner contentment.

If this sounds too worthy for words, it isn't. It's very practical. As is the getting of love. Love is there for saint and sinner alike. Having love in your life is an achievable goal for anyone.

Don't worry if you're out of practice, if the modern world has so alienated you from your true feelings that you don't know where to start. This book has been designed as the dowsing tool that will enable you to trace your own personal supply and, I hope, encourage you to spread a bit of it around.

It will show you how to get so much love into your life you won't know what to do with it all. It will change your perception of reality and your concept of what life . . . and love . . . is all about.

So how *do* you start?

You start with a drop in the ocean. That drop, small as it is, will form a ripple that spreads, in ever widening circles, to encompass lives you've never touched and situations you've never experienced. There is a knock-on effect to love. And like compound interest, it multiplies out of all proportion to the original investment. When you're least expecting it you'll be overwhelmed with a tidal wave of the stuff.

You don't believe it? Well, don't take my word for it. Try it and see. If it *doesn't* work, you'll at least have the pleasure of saying 'I told you so'.

But it *will* work. It always does.

Love, once unleashed, is an overwhelming force. An unstoppable stream. It revives everything it touches and softens even the hardest heart.

Read on.

And find out how to put a little love into *your* life.

LOVE FOR YOURSELF

Chapter I

'Isn't loving myself . . . well . . . selfish?'

No. It isn't. Get that out of your head straight away.

Most of us are brought up to equate self-love with selfishness. In reality they are poles apart. Selfishness is about need, about demanding, about never having enough to fill the black void of emptiness that is where love is not. Self-love is about acceptance, about appreciation, about knowing that, whatever happens, you will always be there for you.

Loving yourself is where it all starts. And yet some of us are so cowed by early conditioning that we would rather put the needs of anyone else, no matter how self-serving or ungrateful, before our own. And then we wonder why we're treated like doormats.

Many of us are so damaged we even have a problem with the words. If 'self' and 'love' linked together make you feel distinctly uncomfortable, it's time you realized that you are still a victim of your early pro-gramming. Childhood memories are hanging around to haunt you. But you are a grown-up now. Being told not to show off or not to be so greedy or that you always think about me, me, me when you are six, has no power over you when you are twenty-six. Unless you give it that power. It's your choice.

You may find it easier to deal with epithets like self-worth or self-esteem rather than self-love. Both concepts are admirable in themselves. But they are essentially passive. Something you have rather some-thing you do. You cannot worth yourself. But you *can* love yourself. Love is an active process. You can give love. And no matter how hard you try, you can-not take it unless it is freely given.

The only thing stopping you from giving love to yourself is fear. Fear that it's wrong, or not quite ac-ceptable. Fear instilled in you when you were too young to know any better. Fear designed to clip your wings and keep you in your place.

If you suspect that you are still harbouring such a fear, here's a simple exercise to help you find out. Go to a mirror. Look into your eyes. Say, 'I love you.'

Most people find this incredibly difficult. Some find it impossible.

You may find yourself unable to hold your gaze. Or you may get angry or feel the whole thing is stu-pid. You might feel the book is a load of tosh and stop right here. Don't. All or any of these reactions are indications that deep down you feel you don't deserve to be loved. This is not only patently untrue, it is also incredibly sad.

We *all* deserve love. And with so much love lying fallow inside, just going to waste, doesn't it make sense to expend some of it on ourselves?

If you equate self-love with selfishness be assured of this. There is a vast difference between loving yourself and the narcissistic hedonism which puts self first.

Self-regard isn't about grabbing or pushing to the front. Loving yourself doesn't mean depriving anyone else. On the contrary, the more you love yourself, the more you will be able to love others. That's the magic formula.

Loving yourself means accepting and appreciating yourself just as you are, not as you feel you 'ought' to be. It means taking time to honour the special, unique human being that is you.

And why not?

You are a miracle in motion, a product of an evolution that has us all descended from, and made up of, the same matter as the stars. Your body is a working wonder, your mind smarter and sharper than the most advanced computer. You are a creator in your own right. Aren't you worthy of love?

You deserve the best that life has to offer. Believe it. So why not cherish yourself as you would any other deserving life form? It's the strongest starting point for getting all the love stored inside you out into the world.

If you find it hard at first, think of yourself as somebody else. Write that alter ego into your 'to do' list or your business diary as you would with any other dependant or contact. Twelve o'clock, lunch with Mary. Nine p.m., bath and gin. This may seem silly but it will focus your attention on how *little* of your time you normally devote to yourself.

Finding a slot in the list or diary may be quite a challenge if you have to juggle the demands of small children, a relationship, a home, a job and/or an ageing relative. But unless you pace yourself, take the occasional breather and nourish your own needs, you will eventually burn out. And that will serve no one, least of all you.

They say work expands to fill the time available, so why shouldn't it contract if you steal a bit of that time for yourself? And since you'll be fresher and better rested, giving yourself a well-earned pause will actually make you more able to devote your best efforts over a shorter period to responsibilities which might otherwise seem to go on for ever. There is no virtue in becoming a drudge and ending up old before your time.

If you don't care for yourself, how can you expect others to care for you? You will gain much more respect if you let people know that you also have needs and desires. You love them, but you are a person too.

Duty, when it is a burden, can weigh heavier than the Ancient Mariner's albatross. So if your role is a cross between chief cook and bottle washer, nanny, chauffeur, odd-job person and skivvy, then it's time you rewrote your schedule to include some quality time for yourself.

If we're talking duty, then always remember that your premier task is to look after you. You deserve nurturing too. If you collapse it won't help the people who rely on you.

Your first task in attracting more love into your life is to cut yourself a bit of slack. Make yourself dispensable. Lower your standards so you can raise your sights.

Some people can't or won't do this. They believe

that they are the only person who can do the job right, whether it is dusting the furniture or filing a report. This is not only arrogance, it is making a stick with which to beat yourself. What does it matter whether a row of carrots is perfectly hoed? In a hundred years' time who will remember (or care) that the family could eat their dinner off the floor of your kitchen?

I'm not suggesting that you live in chaos or send your kids to school with holes in their socks or leave your boss to type his own letters (or if you are the boss, leave your secretary to deal with that awful man from accounts while you take a four-hour lunch break). What I *am* suggesting is that, if you get sick or change your job, or the children leave home, you are doing no one any favours if your dependants are incapable of boiling an egg or finding an invoice.

So delegate responsibility. Wherever you live, wherever you work, teach your children, able-bodied partners and work colleagues to be self-sufficient. And spend the time that is freed up on spoiling yourself.

Simplify your home life

- Don't pick up after anyone. If you can't bear the chaos, keep a big box in a visible position and throw into it everything that hasn't been put away. When your daughter has to disentangle her best sweater from her brother's dirty rugby boots, or your live-in lover discovers that the dye from the damp towels has made an interesting pattern on his/her silk shirt, they'll get the message.

- Make a rota. Everyone can wash dishes, set tables, hoover their own room, empty their own waste-paper basket. This especially if you're in a student house. Even the most inveterate mummy's boy can learn to iron his own clothes and work the washing machine and make his own breakfast of a morning.

- The smallest children can put away their things and make their beds (duvets are a godsend). Once it's a habit they'll always do it. Think how grateful their future partners will be.

- Make rules – and stick to them. No toys in the lounge. Coffee cups back in the sink (hopefully washed up, but this might be pushing it a bit) rather than left all over the house. Dock pocket money or set fines for infringements. Nothing speaks louder than money-deprivation. Not even a clip round the ear.

- Get help. If the communal coffers will run to it, employ a cleaner. Three hours' worth shouldn't break the bank. A professional will do more in those three concentrated hours than you'd do in a constantly interrupted three days. And you have now got at least three hours a week to work on your novel, go for coffee with a friend or finish your thesis.

- If you have teenagers living at home, don't go into their rooms at all. You don't want to know. It will send you into a decline for the rest of the week. And believe it or not, they *like* it like that.

- When the going gets tough – the tough make themselves scarce. If it all gets too much, don't shout, scream or kick the cat. Instead put a big 'DO NOT DISTURB' sign on your bedroom door. Let everyone know that you will be unavailable for whatever length of time it takes to do your breathing exercises, paint your toenails, read a magazine. Don't come out for anything less than the most dire emergency.

- If you are housebound and have children who are too young to be left alone, take time off when they're having their nap. Don't use the welcome break to rush round doing the house-work. Put your feet up. There will always be more housework. Ask yourself, who will do the housework if you have a nervous breakdown?

- Take a tip from a friend of mine. If all else fails, lock yourself in the loo and meditate. She assures me it was the only thing that kept her sane until her husband landed a job with an oil company and they could suddenly afford help with her three hyperactive offspring.

- Never iron anything. Fold bed linen as it comes out of the machine. Hang clothes straight on to hangers. Buy drip-dry shirts and wash and wear everything else. Anyone fussy can do their own if and when the occasion arises.

Simplify your work life

- Cut out travelling time (and hassle). Wherever possible, work from home.

- Just say no. Say no to jobs that are other people's responsibility, or whenever you feel someone is taking advantage of you.

- Let it be known that you will only be available to answer the phone between two and three in the afternoon. Otherwise the answerphone will be on. It's astonishing how much time is wasted during a working day.

- Never take meetings (see above). Call or fax instead.

- Politely refuse to stay late because the boss has given you ten letters to type at 5.25. Say you have a previous appointment. You have. With yourself. Your time is just as valuable as his. If you always do it, you'll always *have* to do it.

- Take your full holiday time and lunch-hour and coffee breaks. Enjoy them. Don't feel guilty. Sit in the sun. Go for a swim. Visit an art gallery.

- If yours is the kind of job where everyone feels obliged to work extra hours or twice as hard (in case they lose the job) and is constantly looking behind them in fear of the knife, it may be time to think about changing your job. If enough people did so, exploitative bosses wouldn't have a workforce to exploit – and serve them right.

- Never work overtime for nothing. Value your time and your efforts. Recognition needn't be in the form of money but nor should it be assumed that you are a worthless dogsbody.

- If someone tells you it will be good experience, beware. They want you to do something diffi-cult, that you will hate, for no reward. Trust me.

Spend the time saved doing things *you* want to do. Use it to nurture yourself, to expand your horizons, to develop your potential. To explore and enjoy your-self, body, mind and spirit.

Why? For the pleasure it gives you and the enjoy-ment you gain. That's reason enough.

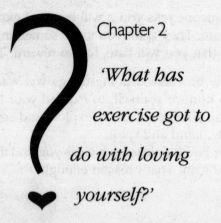

Chapter 2

'What has exercise got to do with loving yourself?'

Plenty. If you think of exercise as a chore, a bore, something to be endured rather than enjoyed, then you've missed the point. Exercising to keep your body in the best possible condition is one of the most loving gifts you can give yourself.

We are talking masters and servants here.

If you have a body that is so deconditioned that you go blue in the face if you have to climb a flight of stairs, that is so stiff you can't stretch or dance or strut your stuff, that you cover up with layers of clothes because you're ashamed to be seen in it, then it is clear that your body is the master and you are the servant. The machine you inhabit is calling the shots. It is dictating the quality of your life.

This is the opposite of what should be the case.

Your body is nothing more than the instrument through which you access the physicality of the world. If you keep that body strong and well serviced then you will be the master and it will do as it's told. It will move with ease and grace, run like a gazelle, power up hills without getting out of breath and lift weights without putting your back out.

A body that functions properly is a joy to inhabit. It makes you feel alive and brim-full of energy. Like you were when you were a kid. And all it demands in return is a little regular maintenance. Only twenty minutes a day will make a tremendous difference.

Regular is the operative word because if you let it all lie fallow for six months then, two days before you go on holiday (and try on your bikini . . . eeek!), decide that it's time to do something about the excess weight, you will be doomed to disappointment. Little and often is the motto with exercise. And it's amazing, once you've got your body in shape, how little effort it takes to maintain the status quo.

Remember you are exercising to enhance your enjoyment of life rather than to win the London Marathon or compete in the National Aerobic Championships. If you want to do either of the latter, far be it for me to dissuade you, but, naturally, if you do, you'll need to train somewhat harder than you would if the object is merely to bounce rather than drag yourself out of bed of a morning.

Exercise is a means to an end, not the end in itself. The end is to feel wonderful. The bonus is that, as a result of your efforts, you will also *look* wonderful. Your posture will improve and your flesh firm up. You may not lose weight because you'll be losing fat and gaining muscle, and muscle weighs more than fat. But muscle also takes up less space than fat, so you'll lose inches.

If you were lousy at games at school and associate exercise with cold knees on freezing hockey pitches, you are probably groaning inwardly and preparing to skip the rest of this bit. Do yourself a favour. Don't. Like a well-tuned car, a well-toned body is much more of a pleasure to drive than something which feels as though it's falling apart at the seams. We are not talking aesthetics here, we are talking comfort and value and the sheer unadulterated joy of having a body that obeys you rather than one which sets constraints on what you do because of its sheer inefficiency. Exercise is an insurance policy that will allow you to live as you were supposed to live, glorying in the machine that you inhabit.

Exercise is a much misunderstood subject and far too complicated a one to cover in detail here – besides which, the shelves are groaning with exercise books, so if you're interested you can get all the info you need elsewhere. But let's just make a few basic points so that you get the best value from your efforts.

First, choose something you know you're going to enjoy. If you're non-competitive, don't take up tennis. If you hate water, avoid the local pool. If you choose an exercise class, make sure it's the right level (i.e. if you've got two left feet you might feel more comfortable doing yoga than modern jazz). If you're shy, go with friends (salsa and line-dancing are fun). Check out the facilities round and about and choose the location in which you feel most comfortable, welcome and at home. Otherwise you won't go. Then choose a time that's convenient – and stick to it.

Second, get educated as to which exercise does

what. A stationary bike won't tone up your bikini bulge. It'll get some more oxygen round your body and tone up your heart muscle but to neaten the waist you'll need to do some toning work.

Third, exercise has to be balanced. To be a totally fit and healthy human being you need to aim for the three S's: stamina, strength and suppleness.

Let's look at them one at a time.

Stamina

To increase your stamina you need to do aerobic exercise. (*Groan.*) This involves using the big muscles (like the quads, down the front of the thighs, or the glutes in the behind) to pump oxygen round the body. Aerobic literally means 'with air'.

Aerobic exercise will help you lose weight (all over, not in spots) and improve your cardio-vascular system (heart and lungs). A really healthy heart, conditioned by regular aerobics, will need to pump fewer times to get the same amount of oxygen round the body. And it stands to reason that the less it pumps, the longer it's going to last. Side-effects of aerobic exercise include an improved circulatory system (to keep you warm in winter), a more efficient immune system (so that you catch fewer colds), stronger bones, healthier teeth, glossier hair and a better skin.

Movements should be rhythmic and continuous (tennis is not aerobic because it stops and starts) and should last for a minimum of twenty minutes per session. Three sessions a week on alternate days is ideal.

Aerobic exercise includes walking, cycling, swimming, jogging and aerobic dance classes. Try to enjoy it. Your efforts will give you *more* energy rather than less, so after a workout you should feel revived and full of beans.

Strength

This involves doing specific exercises to tone and strengthen specific muscles, with or without weights. (A handy weight is a 1 lb. bag of dried haricots or a can of baked beans – just be careful you don't drop the latter on your toe!) Although there are many excellent books on the market which will show you which exercises tone where, it's always a good idea to take a class first so that you get some qualified instruction until you know what you're doing.

Again, three times a week on alternate days (the days you're not doing your aerobics) is ideal. You don't have to do callisthenics continuously. You can fit them in in dribs and drabs any time during your day. I do mine when the commercials are on!

A word of advice. We exercise the muscles in our legs by walking about and those in our arms by picking things up. All we do with our stomachs is fill them with food. So if you only have time for one set of exercises, focus on the stomach and back muscles which will give you a strong internal corset to support the body and stop your waistline from becoming a thing of blessed memory.

By the way, there is no such thing as spot reduction. You cannot lose weight off just one area. What you can do is tighten and tone the muscles in that area (the waist, for instance) so that the body *looks* thinner.

Suppleness

This is the one that everyone forgets but for a balanced body it's every bit as important as strength and stamina. You should stretch out your muscles before you start a workout (to make sure you're not working with tight muscles which can snap – ouch) and again afterwards to avoid post-exercise stiffness (PES).

Again, consult a class teacher or a book for relevant stretches. Long, lean muscles are much more elegant than tight, bunchy ones. And since stiffness makes you look and feel old, you should stretch daily – no matter how old you are.

Exercise doesn't have to be a chore. If it is, you'll give up. Think laterally. Lots of hobbies have a built-in exercise element. Hill-walking. Rambling. Swimming. Golf. Tennis. Badminton. Sailing. Skiing. Cycling. Try to get away from the idea that exercise is a bind. What could be more enjoyable than a long walk in the bluebell woods with a picnic at the end of it? Much better for mind, body and spirit than doing twenty minutes' monotonous movement on a stairwalker.

And you can always try building exercises into the lifestyle. Use every chance you get to climb stairs rather than take the lift. Walk to the shops if you're only going for a couple of items (the way parking is these days you'll probably get there just as quickly). Stretch up for that item on the top shelf rather than asking someone taller to get it down for you.

Think physical and pretty soon exercise will become a life-enhancing habit.

Even if you have let things slide for years (or if you've never done any exercise at all), for heaven's sake don't write yourself off as a lost cause. Life is for living at peak performance. You owe it to yourself to give exercise a try. Whatever your age, sex, profession or lifestyle you can see positive results.

And it's amazing, no matter what state you're in when you start, how fast the body responds when you begin to give it a bit of attention.

I know this from personal experience. I recently tottered off to Spain, having spent the previous three months glued to a word processor six hours a day, seven days a week. I was working to a deadline dictated by my depleted bank balance and, by the time I hit Malaga, I was in a state of disrepair. Not only had I put on weight (a slug had more of a waistline), but that weight was clumped in dimpled lumps around my middle and rear end. My sacroiliac joint was out of whack and I'd done something to my hamstring so that I couldn't sit down for more than ten minutes without discomfort. My eyes were so bloodshot and swollen I could hardly see out of them. All in all, I was not a pretty sight. And I felt about ninety-two. I couldn't walk a hundred yards without getting out of breath and I was as stiff as an old board.

Yet within a few weeks I had shed the weight, regained the energy and looked at least twenty years younger.

And I didn't need to join an expensive health club or hire a personal trainer to effect this transformation. Nor did I need to half kill myself. I was lucky enough to have the use of a pool, and the flat I stayed in was situated at the top of a hill.

My regime was simplicity itself. I swam in the morning, worked out in the afternoon and walked in the evening.

The first day I swam one length. No more! I did

one exercise and a stretch. And I walked down the hill to the shops (thirty minutes down and forty minutes up – with the shopping). On that first walk my knees were wobbly both going down and coming up and I had to stop every five minutes, ostensibly to admire the spectacular view, in reality to get my breath back.

I added one length of the pool and one exercise and stretch per day to my routine. That was all. By the end of two weeks I was swimming fourteen lengths, working out for half an hour and could do the walk down in twenty minutes and the walk up again in twenty-five.

By the time I left, a few weeks after that, my back was better, my eyes had cleared and my lumps and bumps had gone. I was doing forty lengths in half an hour, an hour's workout daily and powering up and down the hill at fifteen minutes each way. Like the phoenix, I had risen from the ashes of sloth. And I didn't feel stiff or exhausted.

Little over a month previously such a regime would have floored me. But the body is a truly wonderful ally. It will rally round with amazing rapidity – provided you don't ask it to do too much, too soon.

Trust it. Listen to it. Challenge it. Own it. Love it. And it will love you back with interest.

Chapter 3

'Why am I never happy with my weight?'

Many reasons. Peer pressure. Brainwashing. The current style for ectomorphic bodies. Lack of self-esteem. But mostly because you're confusing food with love.

Food is not love. If you give yourself enough love, then weight will cease to be an issue.

Food is fuel, nothing more. It can be delicious. It can be destructive. It energizes our magnificent machine. But if we overfill the tank we clog up the engine.

Various foods break down in the body to produce different results. Some foods build bones and teeth, others repair and replace tissue and cells, still others give us the get up and go to . . . well, get up and go. We are constantly renewing ourselves through the food we eat.

Left to its own devices, the body deals wonderfully with this complicated and magical process, taking what it needs, dispersing it to the relevant points of the physical compass, eliminating the rest. If we overload the system by eating too much, it will even store the residue as fat, against the evil day when the supply dries up. That's how much our body loves us.

The problem is that, in the affluent West at least, the supply *doesn't* dry up. Famine and hard winters when the crops froze in the ground are things of the past. So unless we balance the 'energy in–energy out' equation, we will just get fatter and fatter.

The effect is exacerbated by the fact that the metabolic rate, the rate at which we use up our calories, slows down as we get older. This, coupled with a falling off in energy expenditure, leads on directly to the dreaded middle-age spread. Unless we do something to redress the balance. Eat less, exercise more. Energy in, energy out.

Again the shelves are groaning with diet books. Hardly a day passes but some new 'miracle' method presents itself. But dieting is such a negative concept: deprivation writ large.

Anyway, dieting doesn't work. The body goes into a siege situation if it's deprived of food. It assumes that there *isn't* any food and so it moves into self-preservation mode by shifting the metabolism down a gear. However, if we give up the diet, or when we reach our target weight and start to eat normally again, the body, deciding to hedge its bets for a while, takes some time to shift the metabolism up again. Result? What we used to eat to stay at a normal weight now makes us *gain*. Catch-22.

So, the basic, physical reason why people put on

fat is that they eat too much and don't exercise enough. Heavy bones, 'glands', and the fact that it runs in the family, are self-delusionary excuses that delude no one else. As Orson Welles said, 'Gluttony is not a secret vice.'

But with the wealth of nutritional knowledge now available why is it that obesity in the West has reached epidemic proportions?

Simple. Because it's one thing to know what you ought to do to achieve and maintain your target weight – but it's another thing to *do* it. Knowledge without action will not produce results.

Food is a very complicated issue. We do constantly equate it with or substitute it for love. This is not as perverse as it sounds. It goes back to our very earliest memories, when we were suckled at our mother's breast. Even if we were bottle-fed, food equalled warmth, affection, cuddles, attention. If we cried we had something put in our mouths. The hunger and the loneliness went away.

In adulthood, mother's milk is no longer on the menu, so if we feel unloved, many of us dull the pain by eating a biscuit – or if the pain is *very* bad a whole packet. And it works, for a time. The pain eases. Until we look in the mirror and the guilt sets in.

So then what do we do?

Instead of sitting down and asking ourselves what is really bothering us, and doing something about it, we head straight back for the fridge. Avoidance technique. So the problem remains unsolved. Hidden under a barrage of chocolate biscuits until it pops out to trip us up again . . . and again . . . and again.

Some people are so uncomfortable about food they can't deal with it on any level and become anorexic. Bulimics try to keep their weight in check by stuffing themselves to bursting point and then throwing it all up again. Both diseases are driven by lack of self-esteem and a sense of extreme unworthiness. Most anorexics and bulimics will admit to deep feelings of self-loathing. The very opposite of love.

The trouble is, we have to eat to live. Other addictions are at least avoidable. Neither booze nor drugs are necessary to sustain life. With food it's a different matter. We are confronted with it several times a day, day in and day out.

The only way to deal successfully and permanently with the food conundrum is to stop stuffing ourselves and start loving ourselves. If we learn to distinguish between the two and give ourselves the love we deserve we won't *need* to shove chocolate into our faces to feel like valid human beings. We won't be constantly bingeing and purging, dieting and starving. We will be able, at last, to get off the treadmill.

And because our body always has our best interests at heart, our weight will regulate itself at the point that is right for our height, bone structure and age. We will eat when we're hungry and stop when we're full.

My mother tells me that, when I was young, my digestive system seemed to work on a 48-hour cycle. One day I was starving, the next I didn't want to eat much. I was a wiry and energetic child. And luckily my mother was wise enough not to force me to eat on my non-hungry days. If she had, then I would have been overweight and unhealthy.

Which is what I became when I left home in my late teens to go to drama school. Overcome by a fear of my own inadequacy, I put on three stones in as many months. Three stone, I might add, that I didn't lose until I learned to accept myself for who I was and not who I wanted to be (Marilyn Monroe).

The dieting industry rakes in millions every year. Even though the success rate is so low and statistics prove that most people who lose weight through dieting put it all back on again (and then some) within two years, still we fork out our fivers in hope of a painless cure.

Why? Because we want to be glamorous, normal (whatever that is), thin. Because, basically, we want to be loved.

It is also a health issue. Obesity carries with it the risk of furred arteries, heart attack, diabetes, hypertension and early death.

And an image issue. Apart from having to suffer the ridicule and scorn of the less well padded, surveys have shown that overweight people are perceived to be less intelligent than their thinner counterparts.

It's even a career issue. Well-qualified applicants have been refused jobs and/or job insurance solely on the grounds of their excess weight.

All of these issues lead to untold misery and heartache that could be avoided if we indulged ourselves more in the food of love and less in the love of food.

Let me say right here and now that, except for the fact that I don't want to be fat myself – more for the way it makes me feel than the way it makes me look – I have no prejudice against the more voluptuous figure. Human beings are as diverse and individual as snowflakes and, as far as I'm concerned, *vive la différence*. I cannot think of anything more boring than a world full of perfect size tens.

If you are heavy but happy – great. You know the score and if you would rather have a plate of chips than a 26-inch waist that's up to you. Provided you love and accept yourself just as you are, your weight is your own affair.

There has been, of late, a move to make fat 'acceptable', to rail against prejudice, to try to change the public perception of 'big' people. Naturally, a little education wouldn't go amiss. For instance, perhaps the glossy magazines might concentrate slightly less on the waif image. But if you are happy to be large, then it shouldn't matter what anyone else thinks about you. And if you are not happy, then it's up to you to do something about it. You cannot change the world. You can only change yourself. As long as you try to put the blame elsewhere, as long as you refuse to accept responsibility for your eating patterns, the unwanted pounds will continue to cling to your frame.

When you learn to love yourself, warts and all, you will start to listen to your body's messages. And your body will offer you alternatives.

Do you really want a doughnut – or are you bored? Wouldn't it be better to go for a walk in the sunshine (or even the rain)?

Must you have an extra helping of apple pie – or are you cold? Wouldn't it be better to put on an extra sweater?

Is a plate of chips the only thing that's going to get you through the rest of the afternoon – or are you tired? Wouldn't it be better to have a nap?

Are you heading for the breadbin because you're hungry or just because he/she hasn't rung? Wouldn't it be better to put the answerphone on and go to the movies with a friend?

A strange thing happened to me during my Spanish sabbatical. Having been on a fruit fast for a couple of days and having drunk gallons of water to flush out my system and stop myself from getting dehydrated in the heat, I went out to dinner with some friends. I didn't consume a lot – just some fish and a salad and cheese and a couple of glasses of wine. But I found I slept badly and that my digestion was upset. It didn't right itself until I went back into vegetarian mode.

I have always been a carnivore, albeit a hypocritical one. If I had to kill anything personally to eat it, I certainly couldn't – but I have been happy to let someone else do my dirty work for me. But now my body was clearly trying to tell me something. On the vegetarian regime I felt lighter, happier, less clogged up. I had boundless energy and a new incentive to finish the project on which, beforehand, I'd been completely bogged down. My skin and cellulite cleared much faster than I would have expected. And I was hardly ever hungry. When I was, the enormous salads and vegetable dishes satisfied me without making me feel over-full.

I also found myself slotting into that 48-hour cycle again. Hungry one day, not hungry the next. And I had the good sense to emulate my mother's wisdom and listen to rather than reject my body's messages. This is something we could all do more often: listen to our own bodies.

Since I've come back home I have reverted to eating fish and chicken but I've given up dairy foods and red meat without a struggle. And I used to like my steak so rare it was almost walking off the plate.

The experience has taught me not only that I

needn't eat just because it's lunchtime (who made these rules anyway?) but also that food is not something alien that we push in to keep us going. It is part of the cycle of living. And the more natural we make it the better. A salad made from fresh, plump, sun-ripened tomatoes *must* be better for you than a hamburger full of hormones and grease.

I've always known this, of course, but this summer was the first time that I'd experienced it at a cellular level. My body is aware of what's good for it. All I had to do was listen with love.

Giving your body food that sustains and helps it to regenerate is a loving gesture. So maybe food, the right food, living, growing, wholesome and as un-tampered with as possible, *is* love after all.

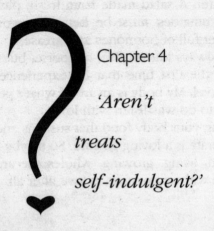

Chapter 4

'Aren't treats self-indulgent?'

Certainly not. Treats are a way to reaffirm that you love yourself.

We all need and *deserve* treats. Not only to break the monotony of daily routine, but to reward ourselves and acknowledge our successes. Too often we strive to achieve something and, having achieved it, don't even take time to thank ourselves for a job well done. We rush on to the next challenge . . . and the next . . . until we burn out or collapse from exhaustion.

Life is about ebb and flow. After a particularly challenging period we need to recover and unwind. To relax and enjoy ourselves. That way we build up the energy to face the next phase refreshed and revitalized. If we don't take breaks we end up running on an empty tank. And no one produces their best work in that condition.

A change of pace, or place, can trigger ideas or send us in directions that would never have occurred to us if we had just followed the old routine. Routine is great for giving shape to the day but it should never become a substitute for life. Routine can hoodwink us into believing that we are getting somewhere when, as Hemingway said, we are just 'confusing action with motion'.

Some ways of behaving become ingrained. If you've got into the habit of opening the fridge door every time you go into the kitchen, it may take a change of kitchen before you can get a grip on your comfort eating. It doesn't have to be a permanent change. A temporary one – a day or two at a friend's house, for example – can be just as effective. Something that makes you aware of the less healthy habits you have fallen into – and shakes you out of them.

Alterations in exercise and diet regimes, like those mentioned in the previous two chapters, are much easier to instigate in a new location. It is the change, as much as the rest, that makes people look and feel so much better when they've been away on holiday.

But we seem to feel that, break-wise, two weeks abroad is all we are owed during the course of a 52-week year.

Is that balance? Fifty weeks' grafting and two weeks' respite? Hardly. Whether it's hereditary, socially ingrained or part of our genetic make-up, we seem to have this unfathomable sense of guilt about treating ourselves well. Why? As long as we're not taking our happiness at other people's expense, what is *wrong* with being happy? Is it more worthy to be miserable? Does it improve the quality of our life – or, indeed, anyone else's – if we are sad?

We need to get rid of the notion that there is something naughty about doing things we enjoy.

For instance, how long is it since you did absolutely nothing?

And I mean absolutely nothing. Not gardening, not hoovering, not watching TV, not reading a magazine – but absolutely nothing. One of the greatest treats in life is to sit on a mountain or in the garden or even on the roof of a summer evening, and watch the world turn from day to night. That hour or so of calm is time well spent. It gives one a sense of perspective, of the endless movement of the planets, of the sheer beauty of the world, of the smallness of our problems.

Treats don't have to be highly organized or incredibly expensive. Watching the sun go down is something any of us can indulge in any time we choose. And it's free. But how many of us think to turn off the mind-numbing virtual reality of the latest soap opera, pour ourselves a nice glass of wine and connect like this with the universe?

Step off the treadmill. Widen your horizons. See the big picture. Otherwise tunnel vision sets in. You forget that life is there to be lived – that you deserve to be loved.

The very best kind of treats are those which are *not* earned or pre-planned, but those that occur spontaneously. An ice-cream bought in the middle of a shopping trip, lunch in the park away from the office on the first sunny spring day, a spur-of-the-moment decision to take a drive. Just for the hell of it. Just because we feel like it.

We all ought to do more of this. Flex our treat muscles. Practise doing things that have no other earthly value except that they give us pleasure. Proof positive that we love ourselves enough to treat ourselves well.

If it's so long since you had a treat that the very thought of one sends shivers of guilt down your spine, here are some ideas to get you started.

Treats

Outings

Have you ever had an interest that you've allowed to lie fallow, or a skill that you've let go rusty? Whether it's a passion for music, the arts, Shakespeare, antiques, rock 'n' roll or foreign travel, now's the time to follow it up. Even the smallest first step can start an avalanche of possibilities.

Perhaps you used to be a theatre buff? If you join the local Theatre Society you will receive advance notice of upcoming productions and be able to book facilities at concessionary rates and attend social events linked to the theatre, like tea with the cast or backstage tours.

If art is your enthusiasm, you can investigate the many galleries and museums which run similar schemes where you get invitations to previews at special prices and/or talks by local artists. They might even run painting classes if you fancy trying it yourself.

Why don't you go to the movies more often? The experience of seeing the Oscar winner on a big screen is altogether more impressive than getting a video out and crashing on the couch. The collective response of an audience magnifies the whole sensation.

If your partner isn't interested (or if you are currently partnerless), go on your own. This is a treat for *you*.

Are you into stately homes and/or gardens? Then try the National Trust. A year's membership is excellent value and gives you cut-rate entrance fees and a choice of holiday homes in everything from a lighthouse to a converted castle.

Join a society. For addresses to do with any particular interest or hobby from photography to bird-watching, look in your local phone book or in the back of specialist magazines. If your newsagent doesn't have any, the library surely will.

Check your local bus company for day trips. Like Londoners who have never been to the Tower of London, we are usually woefully ignorant of the spectacular sites and scenery on our doorstep.

If you live in the South of England, why not hop over to France for a bit of culture shock? Come back loaded with wonderful cheese and wine. Only half an hour by the Channel Tunnel.

Wherever you live in Britain you can at least take a weekend trip to the seaside. Living on an island we are lucky enough never to be too far from the salt sea air. Wonderfully energizing – even in the winter – with all those negative ions. Take loads of books and a warm coat for walks on the prom to blow the cobwebs away. Bring back pebbles and shells to extend the memory.

Provided it will interest, intrigue, inform, or just plain amuse you, do it. And don't be guilty about it.

Home comforts

- Long scented baths.

- Foot soaks in front of the telly.

- A nap in the afternoon.

- An hour on the sun-lounger in the garden with a large gin and tonic.

- A good book. It can alter time and space and totally change your state of mind.

- Breakfast in bed.

Indulgences

- A massage.

- A sauna.

- A stint in a flotation tank.

- A swim followed by a soak in a jacuzzi. The Holiday Inn in Aberdeen used to offer a 'Splosh 'n' Nosh'. For a set fee you could enjoy a swim, a sauna and a jacuzzi and then have Sunday lunch. If you brought the papers and had a cocktail before you ate, you could virtually make a day of it. If you have a similar large hotel in your vicinity you might want to check this one out.

- Mud baths.

- A visit to the hairdresser.

- Anything else you can think of that involves somebody pampering you shamelessly.

- A trip to the park or a ramble through the woods.

- A walk in the rain.

- Love in the afternoon.

Therapy

- Reflexology. Afterwards you'll feel like you're walking on air.

- Any bodywork – Reiki, Rolfing, yoga.

- Restoration and repair. Chiropractic for re-balancing. Osteopathy to tweak away the aches and pains. Shiatzu. Chiropody.

Retreats

If life has been pummelling you to the point where a tiny treat isn't enough, try to get right away from the pressure.

- Go to a health farm for a long weekend.

- Jet off to foreign climes for ten days. Stay in the best hotel you can afford. This is no time for roughing it.

- If you are in a state of total despair then a spiritual retreat may be in order. A non-threatening environment in which to get your head together may be just what you need. You don't have to be religious to take advantage of the tranquillity on offer. (Look under *Retreats* at the back of the book.)

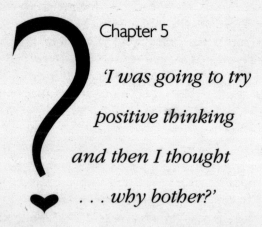

Chapter 5

'I was going to try

positive thinking

and then I thought

. . . why bother?'

You have to bother. The quality of your life depends on it.

One of the most corrosive elements in modern life is the scourge of negative thinking. Expecting the worst. Anticipating disaster. Worrying about the future. Regretting the past. Thinking we're not good enough. Envying another's well-deserved success.

None of these responses serves us. Negativity colours our existence – or rather discolours it, encouraging us to view the world as somewhere huge and horrible over which we have no control. If we think of ourselves as victims of a cruel fate, then we will be. It's as simple as that.

Your mind is a powerful creator. It acts on the thoughts you put into it to produce your version of reality. For instance . . .

If you get up on a rainy morning and decide it's going to be a foul day, your mind will do its best to prove you right. Your miserable face and surly attitude will produce a similar response in everyone you meet. You will spread bad feeling everywhere you go. The day will lurch from bad to worse because you will notice only the negative things about it. You'll forget your umbrella on the bus, your mid-morning coffee will be cold, your date will turn up late – or not at all. If the latter, lucky them, they will miss a totally unpleasant few hours. If the former, you will by then be in such an unforgiving mood that the evening will be doomed to disaster before it starts. It could be the end of a beautiful friendship.

If you get up on a rainy morning and decide this is just what the roses needed and it's going to be a great day – guess what, it will be. Your smiling face will not only produce a similar response from everyone you come in contact with but you will brighten up the lives of countless people in the process. The day will get better and better because you will be focusing on the good things about it. Someone will run after you with your umbrella, your mid-morning coffee will be fresh and hot (because you were nice to the tea-lady), your date will be on time because they can't wait to see you, knowing that, the minute they do, they'll be cheered up. The evening will be a roaring success. It could be the beginning of an even more beautiful friendship.

Two identical rainy days. Two totally different perspectives. Two entirely distinct experiences.

Which life would you prefer?

Change the way you think and you can alter the life you live. Believe it or not – you have that choice.

Choose to view existence as a precious gift rather than a burden to be borne.

Choose to anticipate success instead of failure.

Choose to view people as prospective friends and collaborators rather than as enemies and competitors.

Choose to give things your best shot instead of your least endeavour.

Choose to love yourself enough to be happy.

Most of the thoughts that run through our heads are not even ours. They are other people's misconceptions or prejudices or terrors or rules passed on to us when we were too young to argue or picked up by osmosis.

It's time to start thinking for yourself.

Time to start admitting that the world is a quite miraculously wonderful place, that the rhythm of life has a natural ebb and flow, that without the down times we would never enjoy the ups so much, that people in general are friendly and that, living in the late twentieth century, most of us have never had it so good.

Not much more than a century ago (a mere four generations) many of the things we take for granted in the West simply didn't exist. Life expectancy was half what it is today. Operations were done without the benefit of anaesthetic. Vast numbers of women died in childbirth. Dysentery, diphtheria and small-pox were rife. There were no such things as antibiotics. Foreign travel was the prerogative of the rich. The Wright brothers had yet to conquer the air. Film, TV and radio had not been invented. Nobody had a car or a telephone or a washing machine or a fridge. The vast majority of the population was illiterate. Children as young as six worked twelve hours a day down the mines or in sweatshop factories. There was no central heating, little running water and when the sun went down it was candles or bed. As for entertainment, the only thing you might have to look forward to was the next public hanging. Providing it wasn't your own, of course. Filth and degradation were a normal part of many people's lives. In truth, we don't know we're living.

Of course none of the above means that we should skip through existence like a blinkered Mary Poppins, denying problems when they arise, ignoring the bills until the house is repossessed. No one gets through life totally scot-free. What we do need to acknowledge, though, is that the slings and arrows are opportunities for change and growth, not an excuse to self-destruct. Good fortune is wonderful but when it's summertime (and the livin' is easy) we tend to bask and drift and stagnate. It's in the overcoming of obstacles that we learn and mature and expand.

So, searching for, and believing in, a solution – rather than running around like a headless chicken, whining about why this 'always happens to me' or giving up in despair – will not only get you out of the mess more quickly, it will leave you stronger for the struggle.

Many people are convinced they have no control over their thoughts. They feel they are doomed to be miserable because that's the way they are made: 'I can't help it. I've always been pessimistic. There's nothing I can do about it,' they say. This is simply not true. Once you become aware that *you* are the one poisoning your outlook with negative thinking you can call a halt. You can alter your reality. How? With a simple three-point plan.

1. Tell yourself to stop.

2. Make a conscious choice to say the opposite of what you've been thinking.

3. Do something positive to prove your point.

An example

You are worrying about the next day's meeting at which you are afraid things won't go well.

- Say, 'Stop worrying.' Worrying gets you nowhere.

- Remind yourself that you have prepared your material, you are competent to deliver it and you believe in the project. Tell yourself what a benefit your idea will be to the other parties involved, how lucky they are to be given the opportunity to see you and hear it. Congratulate yourself on arranging the meeting in the first place. Say how much you are looking forward to it. Reassure yourself that fear and excitement reveal themselves in the body in exactly the same place, the pit of the stomach. So those butterflies are actually a delicious sense of anticipation, not nerves at all. Convince yourself that you can't wait to get in there and do your stuff.

- Now go and have a long, relaxing bath followed by a good night's sleep.

Another example

You have come home from work, poured a drink and sat down to relax before dinner. The news is on. It is the usual catalogue of disasters.

- Say, 'I am not watching this.'

- Remind yourself that you live in a country that is at peace, you are not starving, 99.99 per cent of the population was not mugged or murdered or run over or robbed today. You are healthy and happy and free.

- Refuse to be manipulated. Turn off the TV and put on some soothing music, something that won't disturb your digestion of the delicious dinner to come. *Never* eat while watching TV – especially if there is something negative on (and when isn't there?). Drama is conflict and good news is no news and you'll be absorbing negative energy with your food. Focus on what you're doing, be aware of the taste and smell and texture of your meal. Don't overload your body with sensations, otherwise you might as well be eating cardboard.

I'd like to share with you a story that's a particular favourite of mine.

In India an old man was sitting under a shady tree one hot afternoon when the Spirit of Plague passed by.

'Where are you off to?' asked the old man.

'I am going to Benares,' answered the Spirit of Plague, 'where I will kill one hundred people.'

Later the old man heard that five thousand people

had died in the town so, when the Spirit of Plague passed by on its return journey, the old man called to it.

'You lied. You said you would slay only one hundred but you killed fifty times as many.'

'I did not lie,' said the Spirit. 'I slew one hundred. Fear slew the rest.'

In this age of mass communication, of wars and rumours of wars, of wall-to-wall news and venal paparazzi and plane crashes and street gangs and terrorists and famine, we are all in danger of being slain by the *fear* of something happening rather than by the happening itself. The happening might even be a quick, clean death. Death by fear is a long, slow, unnecessary process. Refuse to allow this late twentieth-century plague to turn you into a victim.

Cutting out negative thoughts

• Nowhere is the mind/body connection more in evidence than in the link between negative thinking and disease. Depression and worry (or negative stress) can trigger all sorts of physical responses from irritable bowel syndrome to putting on weight (through comfort eating). They can also eat into our ability to take action to help ourselves until it seems impossible even to get out of bed. At this point the last thing you must do is to pull the covers over your head and give up the ghost. The downward spiral which, left unchecked, may lead to suicidal despair can be reversed by the simple expedient of taking some exercise. This is because exercise releases hormones into the bloodstream which act as natural opiates, elevating not only the energy levels but the feel-good factor in the brain. The time to do this is while you are still in control of the situation and before you need to resort to mood-altering drugs or therapy to pull you out of it. Recognize the danger signals. A brisk walk or a half hour in the gym can stabilize the chemical balance and put you back in control of your mental responses and your good humour.

- Acknowledge that there is no earthly reason why you *shouldn't* be happy or successful or rich or famous. Your negative thinking may be the only thing that's holding you back.

- Realize that there is no such thing as failure. Only lessons to be learned. The worst mistake is not to try in the first place.

- Expect the best.

- Trust (don't hope) that you'll get it. Trust represents faith in the positive outcome. Hope usually means that you don't really believe in the result.

- Don't worry . . .

    . . . about the past. You cannot change what's been done. What you *can* do is resolve not to do it again – whatever it was. Then let it go.

    . . . about the future. The only way you can change the future is by what you do now.

. . . about the present. This moment is all you have. Make the most of it. You will never get it back.

- Smile . . . and watch the world smile with you. Better still, laugh. Buy a joke book. Take in a funny movie. Enrol in a laughter workshop (see the back of the book).

- Avoid negative people. So-called friends who spend their time complaining, whining, finding fault, seeing the worst in every situation and generally bringing you down are friends you can do without, at least until you have got to a point of strength and wisdom where their negative attitudes no longer have power to control your reality. There's no need to be rude or unkind. Lie a little. Say you're going away or working hard and can't be disturbed for the time being. When you've achieved a better balance in your own life you may want to tell them gently why you've been avoiding them. Most people have no idea that they're being negative. It's like they're on automatic moan. Who knows, a word from you might start *them* on a new direction that will change their life for the better.

- Look on every problem as a challenge. Search every negative situation for the positive solution and the lessons that you are meant to learn. Then learn them.

- Have faith that everything that occurs is happening for your highest good, and that you will see the point in the long run.

- Turn off the news. Cancel the papers. If something cataclysmic happens you'll learn soon enough. If not, why worry over things that are beyond your control or that don't impinge on your reality day to day?

- Just say yes. To life. To opportunity. To new people, places and things.

Finally, love yourself enough to be positive about the person you are. Your prospects, your talents, your looks, your skills, your successes.

Write a list of all the good things you have going for you. Stick them on your bathroom mirror. Look at them each morning while you're shaving/making up. Start each day in anticipation of the good things in store.

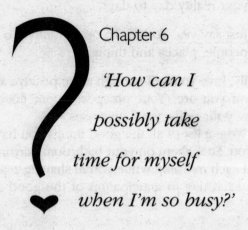

Chapter 6

'How can I

possibly take

time for myself

when I'm so busy?'

Two wise sayings

1. Don't sweat the small stuff – and remember, it's *all* small stuff.

2. Relax. You'll never get out of here alive.

One of the great scourges of the late twentieth century is stress. And although stress reveals itself in various physical ailments – psoriasis, asthma, ulcers, heart problems, hypertension and cancer, to name but a few – it is predominantly a mental affliction. It comes from having too many things on your mind.

Overloaded

Too much to do, too little time. So many demands on your attention that you don't know where to start. And when you *do* start you can't do anything right because you are so busy thinking about all the other things that you should be doing, that won't get done if you don't hurry up, that will still be there when you finish the current task – exhausted – that you can't concentrate on what you're supposed to be doing right now.

This is stress.

And whether it is self-inflicted (by taking on too much) or thrust upon you (by insensitive superiors or demanding relationships), loving yourself means getting a grip on it and calling a halt to the downward slide into distress. Otherwise you end up . . .

Overwhelmed

This is the point at which normal functioning ceases. It's also known as having a nervous breakdown.

In its passive form (driven by despair), it means that everything becomes so much of an effort that it's too much trouble to get out of bed. People in this state often don't wash or clean their teeth. They have totally lost respect for themselves and they simply can't see the point in anything.

In its active form (driven by frustration), people beat their children or stab their spouses, or go up to a high tower with a powerful weapon and shoot everything in sight.

The time to stop being overwhelmed is before it

starts. By recognizing what's happening while you're still in the overloaded stage. By honouring yourself enough to offload everything that doesn't serve you or add to your happiness.

At its most drastic this may mean changing the job or getting out of the relationship. Less desperate situations will respond to the following coping strategies.

Perspective

Stand back and look at the situation objectively. Ask yourself whether you *have* to do whatever it is *this minute*. Chances are, you don't. Will the world come to an end if you don't finish the report by Thursday night? Is the boss away till the end of the week? Will he even get round to reading it until Monday? Certainly not if he's playing golf on Friday.

Psychology

If it really can't wait, then try a little psychology on yourself. Tell yourself that you *choose* to do it, not that you *have* to do it. This may seem simplistic, but it's amazing how changing a single word can alter one's attitude. 'Have' means something is being imposed, over which you have no control. 'Choose' puts you back in control. In doing so it relieves a great deal of the mental pressure.

Lists

Lists are life-savers. They clear your head of unwanted rubbish, leaving your brain free for more enlightened stuff than 'don't forget the dry cleaning'. They also make sure you remember the things you have to do – like picking up the dry cleaning.

To be an efficient list-maker you'll need . . .

- Two diaries. A large desk job which gives you an overview of the week and a mini version in which you can note down phone numbers, appointments or information on the hoof.

  The desk diary can be used as a mini filing cabinet. Slot in bills when they need to be paid, reminders to buy birthday cards – and post them – the day before the birthday. Also, obviously, to record appointments and dates.

  The small diary relieves you of the extra stress factor of having to keep track of innumerable stray pieces of paper upon which you can never put your hand when you need that crucial address. A word of warning though. Make sure you transfer anything important from your mini diary to your desk diary the moment you get in. Otherwise you're going to find yourself double-booked somewhere along the line.

- Scribble pads. In the kitchen, by the phone, on your desk.

- Post-it notes – to stick to the bathroom mirror, on the fridge, on your word processor. Don't just tie a knot in your hanky. If you're suffering from stress overload you're guaranteed to forget what it's there to remind you about. Anyway who carries a hanky any more?

Do it now

Answer mail immediately, preferably with a note or a phone call. Longer letters can be set aside till the afternoon. Otherwise, why wait? Get it done.

Similarly if you have a sudden flash of inspiration or see something in the paper that you want to follow up or buy, act straight away. It's one less thing to distract you and clog up your brain cells.

Breaks

Routine is great but don't let it become another stress inducer. Just because you've made a list doesn't mean you have to finish it today. You can always do it tomorrow. If a thing isn't done by day three, and a major crisis hasn't ensued, cross it off. You either don't *want* to do it or you don't *have* to do it. Let it go.

Get out of the house or office occasionally for a change of scene and perspective. Every so often, fix a day of rest and reassembly. One day off to squander on yourself.

Just say no

Don't rush to help when other people try to offload their chores on to you. Let them have their own nervous breakdown.

Learn to relax

Relaxation is a gift that calms the mind, soothes the body and nourishes the spirit. It's the best possible way to defeat mental scribble, and a skill that can be learned. If you haven't the first notion where to start and the last time you felt relaxed was in your mother's womb, then you may need a little coaching.

Treat yourself to a tape or a book or a class on the subject. Or take up yoga or t'ai chi, both of which emphasize the importance of a quiet mind as well as a supple body.

To relax at home, choose a quiet time and a place where you know you won't be disturbed. Take the phone off the hook. Draw the curtains. Turn off the lights. Put on some soothing music. Lie down flat on the floor in a warm room, with some pillows at your head and feet, and simply unwind. Even five minutes like this in the middle of a busy day can mean the difference between coping and collapsing.

If you fall asleep while relaxing then you're not mentally stressed – you're physically exhausted. You need to get to bed earlier. Relaxation is a kind of mental twilight where, even though you are still aware, your systems are wound down to the point where they can rest and renew themselves in peace.

Relaxation is a powerful tool whose full benefits are only now becoming appreciated by the medical fraternity. Studies currently being undertaken at Aberdeen's Royal Infirmary are likely to show that cancer victims taught relaxation and mental imagery have a better chance of remission and enhanced quality (and length) of life than those left to their own devices after surgery. Deep relaxation apparently triggers the body's immune responses, thus helping patients in recovery to help themselves.

Enter the eye of silence

Nowadays we live our lives under a constant bombardment of noise. Boomboxes and traffic, muzak and pneumatic drills batter us like aural hail, day in, day out.

What we need in the midst of this barrage is some peace and quiet to give our fevered brains a break. Yet it seems that silence is what many of us dread. As if, in that quiet moment, we might be confronted by some terrible secret that the noise is drowning out.

But it is only in silence, in calm, in tranquillity, in what my mother calls 'head-ease', that our minds are void enough to accept the leap of imagination, the spark of intuition, the truly original concept, the essence of who we are.

So clear your mind. Relax your body. It's the loving thing to do.

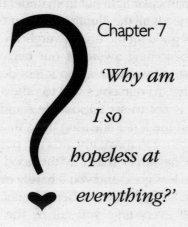

Chapter 7

'Why am I so hopeless at everything?'

If you think you are hopeless and helpless, guess what – you will be. If you think you are capable and efficient – you'll be that too. One set of thoughts dooms you to failure, the other spurs you to success. As the old saying goes, 'If you think you can, or you think you can't – you're right.'

So we're back to the master and servant again. Take control of your thoughts or they will take control of you. Direct your mind to serve you to best advantage. Don't let it run riot like an unruly child, spoiling your day, ruining your life.

Take back your power.

Thinking you're a bad person *disempowers* you. It's not productive and it's not loving.

Loving yourself means accepting all the things

you are, good and not so good. We are far too quick to point the finger of blame at ourselves and desperately slow to congratulate ourselves when we've done something brave or unselfish.

Get your particular light out from under that bushel. The world needs all the illumination you can spare.

Nobody is good all the time. Everybody has their off days. By becoming aware of our behaviour we can take one step towards making it less destructive, more supportive, to ourselves and to others.

The trick is not to set impossible standards and not to focus on the less endearing traits that we may possess. Always try to move towards the positive and away from the negative. That way the good will gently ease out the less good and you'll hardly even know it's happening. Struggling to be better, mentally castigating yourself every time you fall by the wayside, has a way of concentrating the mind on those very aspects you are trying to eliminate.

Loving yourself is a learning process. And since the carrot is always more effective than the stick in producing lasting change, below are some ideas on how to learn to love yourself better.

Accept yourself

Start now. This minute. Don't wait for some mythical tomorrow when you are good, slim, successful, rich. Most people think that they can't begin to love themselves until they're perfect. This is putting the cart before the horse. We will none of us ever be perfect. We can only strive to be the best we can be. Love yourself now, as you are. It's enough.

Promote yourself

In the movie industry they call this 'talking a project up'. Your life is your project and you are its star. Talk to yourself as though you were trying to sell yourself to Spielberg. Use every occasion you can to rhapsodize about your thick, shiny hair, your long lissom legs or whatever you consider to be your best points. And don't dismiss your more idiosyncratic features as ugly. They are what make you an individual. Special. Unique. If you have a problem with your nose – think of Barbra Streisand. That nose (as much as that voice) has made her one of the biggest players in Hollywood and one of the richest women in the world. You think she didn't get teased at school?

Believe in yourself

Think of all the things you do well – your skills and aptitudes and talents and abilities. Now write them down. Stick the list on the dressing-table mirror so that you see them often. Remember that ability has nothing to do with education. Education may enhance an already latent talent but it cannot supply you with a kind nature or a loving heart. List *everything*, no matter how trivial it may seem . . . having green fingers is as valid a skill as being a whizz on the stock market.

Educate yourself

If lack of education is what's holding you back and making you feel unworthy, then go back to school. There have never been more opportunities or options. Whatever your age you can find a class or a course or even a full-time college education if you are determined to do so.

There is a wealth of material in books and on disk at your local library. Make use of it. The more people do, the less likely we are to lose this precious resource to government spending cuts.

Most local councils run adult education classes where you can do anything from carpentry to conversational Catalan. Learn a skill. Get a qualification. Or simply feed your mind with information for its own sake. You'll also open up your social circle with a group of new friends; friends with whom you have something in common straight away, if only the subject you are all studying.

If your ambition is to study full time, call your local college or university and ask about access courses, grants and bursaries.

Life is a learning zone. Open your mind to wider horizons and explore your full potential.

Inspire yourself

Dare to follow your dreams. Don't dismiss your aspirations out of hand as unworkable or overblown. Dream BIG. It's the only kind of dream that will galvanize you into action, encourage you to get up off your butt and try to turn the fantasy into reality.

By all means daydream about your dream. We all do this when we are children. Usually, we are castigated for not concentrating, often on something boring like algebra. As though algebra were any more practical than planning to get to drama school or buy your own restaurant some day. Constructive daydreaming is to be encouraged. Get your dreams out into the ether and start a chain reaction with the universe (read about creative visualization in Chapter 9).

Visualizing your dreams may give you some idea about how you might start realizing them. Perhaps you need to gain more knowledge or save up for some equipment or get some experience that will help you towards your goal? Follow this up and you'll have moved the dream out of your head and into the physical world.

Dreams are good. If you are living a life that's just OK, dare to dream of something better. Much better. Love yourself enough to dream the best for yourself. You may well get it.

People have surmounted impossible obstacles to realize a dream. Why not you?

Empower yourself

Do it by taking each moment as it comes and making that moment rich.

Be true to yourself in the choices that you make. And make those choices pro-active ones. The point of power is in the present. How you look and feel in the future depends on what you choose to do now. Do you study or do you loaf? Do you eat salad or pig out on ice-cream?

And when you make positive choices congratulate yourself. Reinforce the whole process. If you do something well, reward yourself – even if it's only by a word of acknowledgement. Don't say, you could have done better. Where's the love in that? If you are constantly finding yourself wanting, you'll lose faith in your ability to reach the impossible standards you are setting for yourself.

Make it easy to be pleased with yourself, hard to be disappointed. If you make mistakes or don't live up to your promises don't put yourself down. Ask yourself what you learned from the experience. Learn the lesson. Then move on – to the next moment and the next choice.

Laugh at yourself

We all take ourselves way too seriously. Lighten up. We're human, subject to the ills, the foibles, the frailties that all flesh is heir to. It's part of our charm. And although this doesn't give us the right to behave abominably as a matter of course, we could, at least, appreciate the ridiculous in the human condition rather than constantly harping on about the tragedy of it all.

Honour yourself

Never apologize for things which you haven't done or which aren't your fault, just to gain approval. Nobody likes a doormat.

Above all, never apologize to yourself.

If you've done something you're ashamed of,

don't sweep it under the carpet. Acknowledge it, resolve not to do it again, and get on with your life. Undermining your sense of self-worth will only exacerbate the problem. You'll say, 'What's the point? I'm too weak-willed, I'll never succeed.' Instead, your momentary slip will turn into a slide and your worst fears will be confirmed. You never *will* succeed.

Telling yourself you're a bad person is failing to accept yourself. It's self-defeating. If you see yourself as a bad person you'll give yourself licence to do bad things. Change the image to that of a good person who occasionally isn't as good as they'd like to be (i.e. a person who makes mistakes). A good person is less likely to behave badly the next time round.

Of course if you've hurt someone else you *must* apologize. As soon as possible. And mean it. Where others are concerned, love is *always* having to say you're sorry.

Value yourself

If you are put upon by all and sundry, friends and enemies alike, then you may need to enrol in an assertiveness course to shoe-horn you out of habitual behavioural responses that are allowing people to treat you like that.

Assertiveness is different from aggression. In fact it's the opposite. It involves stating your point of view clearly and concisely – and sticking to it. It isn't about scoring points or making your partner, spouse or employer look small. It's about win/win situations, negotiation and ultimately getting what you want.

It comes in handy when dealing with officious bureaucrats, unhelpful shop assistants and disruptive teenagers. It allows you to state your truth firmly and fairly. It will earn you respect, in others' eyes and in your own.

Many councils and education authorities are running assertiveness courses these days. Check your nearest library to see if they have any information on the subject. If there are no local options, ask why not. It'll be your first step in self-assertion.

Enlighten yourself

Consider this book a mere taster in the cornucopia of self-development material that is currently on offer.

If you are already a fan, continue to read and explore. Each insight that you gain leads you a few steps further along your own particular spiritual path. Even if you find that the information in various publications overlaps, don't think that your buying or borrowing them was a waste of time. Repetition reinforces. You cannot hear this kind of material too often – just as you cannot love yourself too much.

Devour whatever books you come across. Listen to tapes. Take classes or workshops to broaden your outlook. We use, on average, only the minutest part of our mental capacity. Like a great iceberg, so much more lies beneath the surface. Love yourself enough to say, 'I matter.'

Because you do.

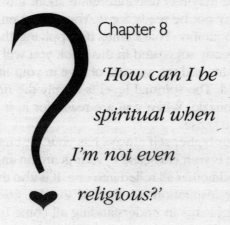

Chapter 8

'How can I be

spiritual when

I'm not even

religious?'

Religion and spirituality are two distinct concepts. There are many different forms of religious worship but all of us, zealot and atheist alike, have a spiritual centre which connects us to our higher self.

In this age of machinery and materialism, this spiritual connection has almost been severed. The cutting of the umbilical cord between body and soul has not served us well. In fact the psychoanalyst Jung stated that, in practically all of the patients he saw over the age of thirty, the malaise could be traced back not to a mental but to a spiritual source. It was, he said, a kind of hunger, a grieving for the loss of 'god', whatever the individual perceived that to be. It was an affliction which he believed to be affecting the whole of mankind and which he felt could only be cured by a collective reconnection with our source.

Getting in touch with your higher self is a way of pushing the envelope of love out beyond the physical barriers of body and mind and into another dimension. That of spirit.

You may feel uncomfortable about this concept. You may not be ready for it. You may even feel it is mumbo-jumbo. That's fine. By applying the principles already suggested in this book you will improve the quality and the amount of love in your life a hundredfold. The spiritual level is simply the final piece in the puzzle. When you are ready for it, it will start to make sense.

Your higher self always has your best interests at heart. It is your conscience, your guardian angel, your fairy godmother all rolled into one. It is also the source of your inspiration. Flashes of insight, good ideas, quantum leaps in understanding all come from your higher self. And it doesn't matter whether you believe in it or not. It believes in you.

One of the ways to start getting your head round the idea is to begin developing your intuition.

Some of us are more naturally intuitive than others. But almost all of us have had flashes of awareness at some time in our lives. Feelings of unease about a situation which later proved dangerous or uncomfortable. *Déjà vu*, where we are sure we have been somewhere or done something before. Unexplainable moments out of real time that leave us dazed and disorientated but somehow exhilarated too. As though we had pulled aside a veil and caught a glimpse of one of the great mysteries.

Some of us are receivers. Some of us are senders.

If you get a sudden urge to call someone and when you do they say, 'I was just picking up the phone to call you,' then you are a receiver. You heard their thought in advance.

If you call someone up and they say, 'I was just thinking about you,' then you are a sender. They have heard your thought in advance. Of course if they also know what you're going to say before you say it, then they're open to two-way traffic.

One of the ways to start developing intuition and thus strengthen the spiritual connection with life, the universe and everything, is to begin to listen. Really listen. To your thoughts, your instincts, your inner dialogue.

To do this you will need to take time to learn to relax and empty your head, then pay attention to the thoughts that pop in unbidden. Take these as a connection to your higher self which is trying to tell you something. The message may seem trivial but there's usually a truth in there somewhere. As you become more adept at listening, so you will become more skilful at deciphering the dialogue.

As your antennae become more sensitive so you will start noticing instances of . . .

Synchronicity

This is where things happen in different places at the same time.

It's as though the universe, in its determination to get the thought out, sends as many mental sperm into the collective consciousness as it can. One of them is going to fertilize the egg that will eventually be born as a fully fledged concept.

Which brings us to . . .

Channelling

Channelling is the ability to allow ideas to flow through you into the outside world. The best creative minds channel ideas – on to paper, into paintings, as musical scores. Write down your ideas and they will take on a reality.

We've all heard of characters in a book 'taking over' from the author part way through the story. I have personal experience of this phenomenon and it's as exciting as it is weird – almost like automatic writing.

Which brings us to . . .

Using the unconscious mind to solve problems

Sometimes we are beset by a challenge so convoluted in its complexity that it seems we will never find a solution. Every avenue leads to a dead end and worrying only makes it worse.

Next time this happens to you try letting the subconscious solve it for you. Offer the problem up before you go to sleep and say you'd like an answer. Ten to one the solution will be there when you come to in the morning. The conscious mind frequently works from a position of total logic. The subconscious has no such restrictions. So the answer that presents itself may be a much more imaginative one than you would ever have worked out in your waking hours.

Which brings us to . . .

Dreams

Dreams often make us aware of problems that we don't want to admit are there in the first place. Deep-seated sources of dis-ease that colour our judgement or cloud our responses . . . may reveal themselves as we sleep.

Listen to your dreams.

Some of them may have straightforward linear forms in which normality still dominates. Others are played out in myth and metaphor.

If you have been having a series of particularly vivid dreams (or nightmares) or, more importantly, a recurring dream, then see if you can use it to divine the message that your higher self is trying to send you. Dream dictionaries are available if you need help with interpretation.

Which brings us to . . .

Insight

Often an idea larger than ourselves triggers a sea change in our mindset. Insights, which may be obscured by physical reality, are truths about the nature of the bigger picture and our place in it.

Insights are a gift from the gods. Listen to them. There are always pointers to our highest good.

Which brings us to . . .

Coincidence

As you begin to open your intuitive channels you will find that the frequency of coincidence increases.

You are looking for a new flat and someone asks you if you know where they can find a tenant.

You decide to take a self-development course and an advertisement for classes leaps out of the paper at you.

You have been toying with the idea of moving jobs and someone offers you a better position.

You wonder what happened to an old friend and you suddenly bump into him on the street.

There is no such thing as coincidence. There is merely an unfolding of your connection with the collective consciousness. Your higher self has begun to manipulate the giant chess game of fate to move those pieces across the board that are to your best advantage.

Which brings us to . . .

Hunches

Listen to your hunches. This doesn't mean you should go out and blow the housekeeping on lottery tickets. But if you have an urge to do something out of character or a feeling that you should be at a certain place at a certain time, don't dismiss it out of hand.

Acting in a new way may open your mind to a new route. Being somewhere strange at a particular moment may bring you into contact with someone whom you might otherwise not have met. Either of these things may set off a chain of circumstances that could turn your life around.

On the other hand, never ignore that niggling feeling that you 'shouldn't' do something. Whether it's buying a new house, changing careers or getting involved with an apparently perfect lover, check and double-check that there aren't hidden loopholes in the deal.

Love yourself enough to trust what your higher self is trying to say. Remember that it is viewing the overall game-plan from an altogether more elevated position. It can see perspectives that we might only glimpse through the parallax view of . . . a hunch.

None of the above has anything to do with superstition, which works through fear. The higher self always works through love.

Which brings us back to . . . *listening* again. The full, protective circle.

Listen to your heart. It won't steer you wrong.

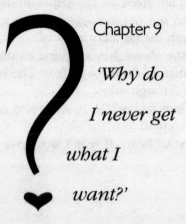

Chapter 9

'Why do I never get what I want?'

Probably because you don't ask.

People aren't mind-readers. If you don't ask, you don't get.

Maybe you think it's wrong to ask because you feel it's selfish? Maybe you're afraid to ask, in case people won't like you? Maybe you're reluctant to ask, because they might think it's too much trouble? Or perhaps you simply don't want to be beholden?

Not asking is a way of denying yourself, of not honouring your worth. Once you start loving yourself, you'll find it much easier to ask and much easier to get.

You'll be astonished at how much you *do* get simply by asking. Most people are only too happy to see you happy. It makes them feel good.

If you have a real block about asking for something for yourself, turn the thing on its head and consider that you are doing the giver a favour. Think of the warm glow you get when you do someone a good turn. Not allowing others that kind of pleasure is a form of selfishness on your part. A way of weighting the balance to your advantage. A control mechanism. They didn't do you a favour? – OK, so they still owe you. You're ahead of the game.

So ask for the favour. And when someone says, 'What would you like to do?' don't say, 'I don't mind, you choose,' and then fume when they pick something you don't want to do. Tell them. Say, 'I'd like to go to the park, or the pub, or Paris for the day.' And *enjoy* it.

Don't think you have to pay back either. Saying thank you and being happy is all that's required.

Of course, in order to get what you want you also need to *know* what you want. Be clear on this. Vague ideas of 'more money', 'security' or 'a better place to live' are usually not enough to galvanize you or the universe into action. You need to be more precise.

This is where using your imagination comes in. Here are some techniques to help you push the business on.

Creative visualization

Creative visualization is a very powerful tool for prising what you want out of life. It's simplicity itself. All you need is some free time, a quiet place and a dream.

The dream could be anything from winning an Oscar to trekking in the Himalayas.

Start by finding your place and your time and settling down quietly and comfortably. Relax your body and clear your mind.

Now begin to fill the empty space with your dream. Try to make it as sharp as possible. Be clear on every detail. If you want a cottage in the country with roses round the door, visualize it as though it were a black and white movie. Then add Technicolor and stereophonic sound.

Is your dream-home made of stone or brick? Is it thatched or tiled? Has it got mullioned, sash or bay windows? How many chimneys does it have? How many rooms? Is there a picket fence? A garden? Are the roses pink or red? Is it in the middle of a meadow or by the edge of a brook? Maybe it's perched on a headland with the waves dashing on the rocks below? Feel the ebb and flow of the tide in your bones.

Walk inside your creation. Picture each room in detail. The size. The shape. The height of the ceiling. The colour scheme, the curtains, the furnishings. Are there flowers, pictures, candles? Is there a four-poster bed? What about the kitchen and the bathroom? Is there a jacuzzi? A sauna?

You can have anything you want in your dream. So set your sights high. If you dream a small dream and you get only half of it, it won't be worth much. If you dream a BIG dream and you get only half of that, it'll still be twice as much as you would have got if you got *all* of your small dream.

Try to make your fantasy as vivid as you can. Bring in all your five senses to help you. See the sun shining through the windows. Smell the roses. Hear the blackbird singing in the garden. Feel the texture of the polished oak table against your fingertips. Take a pear from the fruit bowl and taste the juicy softness of it against your tongue.

Be conscious of how all these things make you feel. You are creating reality in your head. If you create it well enough it should engender the same level of happiness you would get if it were all there on the physical plane. Allow yourself to be happy. You can always be a winner in your dreams.

Another valuable use of creative visualization is to clear away the dross of unhappy memories.

Imagine yourself in a cinema, watching an incident unfold in which you came out badly.

Surround the screen with light. You are the director, scriptwriter and producer of this movie and you're about to rewrite the plot. Whatever the painful memory was, change the dialogue and action to give it a happy ending. You did get the job. You were picked for the team. Your mother didn't scold you or tell you you were bad.

In working through this kind of restructuring of the past, try not to use revenge as the driving force. Forgive and forget – let everyone live happily ever after.

But back to the dream.

Never think of creative visualization as a waste of time. At the very least it will give you a few moments of happiness. At the very best it will get you so clear on what it is that you do want that you start to take the steps that will lead to the dream becoming reality.

You will start to manifest what you desire.

Manifesting

There is nothing magical about manifesting. We all do it, all the time. If you run out of toothpaste and decide you need some more, you manifest it by trotting off to the chemist, plonking down your money and getting a new tube.

Purchasing is one of the simplest forms of manifestation. You took something from your thought life (I need more toothpaste) and brought it on to the physical plane (now I have an actual tube in my hand).

By clarifying what you want in detail you are beginning that process of manifestation. You can start to plan the steps you need to take to get to the dream. No dream is too big to realize if you want it badly enough and are willing to put in the effort to get it.

But there is another, more metaphysical aspect to manifesting. In getting clear, in creating your vision and in affirming your belief in its possibility, you trigger something in the subconscious which begins to manifest the dream on another level of reality. Those coincidences that we spoke about in the last chapter start to happen. People, places and things materialize to help you on your way.

The universe kicks in to give you a hand in the building of your dream. The universe wants you to be happy. It has your best interests at heart. The universe loves you. And as your dream begins to unfold, you'll find it easier to love yourself.

A word of warning. The dream may not unfold in exactly the way you anticipate. Be open to alternatives. If you keep watching the front door, opportunity may knock on the back and you may miss it.

And a word of advice. If the dream seems to be taking for ever to manifest, this may not be the right time for you to get it. You may not be ready for it. Your dream might carry a load of side-effects with it that you are not yet psychologically strong enough to deal with. The universe loves you enough to deny you too, if the dream is not one that would serve your higher good.

Maybe the universe has you marked down for something even *better*?

If your gut feeling tells you that the dream is right for you, don't give up hope. Keep visualizing. Keep taking the steps in the physical world that will bring it closer to fruition. You'll find that as you evolve, so will your dream.

'Follow your bliss,' as Joseph Campbell said. You'll get there in the end.

While you're working towards your dream – and, I hope, enjoying the process (getting there being half the fun) – you can reinforce your resolve through . . .

Affirmations

Affirmations are positive statements about how you would like things to be – as though they already were.

Always state your affirmations in the present tense. Say, 'I have a wonderful cottage in the country,' rather than, 'I am going to have a wonderful cottage in the country.'

The subconscious believes what you tell it, whether it is true or not. So if you tell it you already have something it will try to make sure that you do. 'Going to have' could mean any time in the next millennium.

Saying you have something also strengthens your

resolve and gives you more of a sense of the actuality of the event or object. You will get a feel for what it is like to do the thing or own the item. If you feel prosperous, you are more likely to look prosperous and therefore become prosperous. Very few people are willing to take a chance and lend money to someone who seems to be desperate for a handout. If you look like you don't need it, you'll get it. So try acting . . . as if you had the money, the house, the partner of your dreams. Certainty relieves the tension, makes you less needy.

Let go of the neediness.

Then take the first step in turning your affirmations into truth. Bring them into the physical dimension by writing them down on paper. Stick them all over the place, where you will see them at every turn.

And while you're at it, write one more affirmation. Keep it with you always. Look at it often.

'I love myself.'

And believe it.

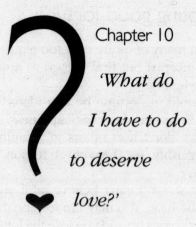

Chapter 10

'What do I have to do to deserve love?'

You don't have to *do* anything. Just *being* is enough. If you still haven't grasped this concept then you might need to go back to the beginning of this book and start again. You've obviously missed the point. The point is that you are lovable and deserving just as you are.

Learn that lesson and you will not only be able to ask for your good, you will be able to appreciate it, guilt free, when it arrives.

Perhaps the most important aspect of loving yourself is being able to accept your good with enthusiasm and grace when it comes along. Acceptance closes the metaphysical circle and allows you to begin to channel the love you're receiving back out into the world again.

By denying your good through an inability to accept, you are turning away the precious gift of love and breaking the cycle of giving and receiving.

Accepting good fortune

Why is it that many of us are only too ready to accept bad luck as normal but find it hard to embrace the concept of winning?

Why should misfortune be considered the 'way things are'? Everyone deserves happiness. And provided that we don't hurt others in attaining it then there's no earthly (or heavenly) reason why we shouldn't have it.

So don't shout 'I can't believe it,' if you have a stroke of good luck. You may nip fortune in the bud. Your number comes up and you lose the lottery ticket. Ouch. You didn't believe it? OK, so you don't get it.

If you truly believe that something is 'too good to be true', it will be. Your belief in yourself, your worth, your deservedness is all part of the equation of abundance. Your gratitude plays an important part in keeping the ball rolling.

Language like 'this can't be happening to me', 'I feel like it's a dream and I'm going to wake up', implies a strong belief in your lack of worth. It's a negation of your right to happiness. And it doesn't serve you. It can repel the good that is out there waiting for all of us.

Giving is easy. Taking is the real test. Can you do it without feeling devalued or beholden or embarrassed? If not, you need to work on your acceptance skills. Loving yourself means being able to receive, secure in the knowledge that you are worthy of the gift.

So open up to abundance with gratitude and joy. Otherwise the flow may slow down to a trickle and the river eventually run dry.

Accepting gifts

If you give someone a present, which would you rather – that they fell upon it with shrieks of delight, ripped off the wrapping and shouted, 'Oh *great*, it's just what I always wanted' or that they set it aside for later and said, 'Oh, really, you shouldn't have'?

Which response is most likely to make you want to give to that person again? Giving and receiving should benefit both parties. Delight all round.

Next time you receive a gift, be generous with your appreciation. And try not to spoil the moment by thinking, oh God, now I have to buy them something back. Being grateful, saying thank you – and meaning it, is good enough.

Give to yourself as often as you can. Treating yourself is a way of demonstrating to your subconscious that you are worthwhile. Reward yourself with a treat today. Just for being you. If you're short of ideas turn back to Chapter 4.

Treats don't have to be extravagant. Set the world an example by cherishing yourself, then stand back and watch the world follow suit.

Accepting compliments

If you've just bought a new dress (or suit) and you know you look the business in it and someone tells you so, don't spoil the compliment by saying, 'Oh, this old thing.' Agree with them. Say, 'Isn't it great? I just love it.'

Similarly, if you've done a good job and someone praises you, don't say anyone could have done it. Maybe anyone could. But the point is that you did it. Say, 'I'm really pleased too,' and mean it.

Accepting love

When someone wonderful whom we fancy like mad falls in love with us there's always the temptation to wonder whether they need their eyes or their head examined.

'How can they possibly love me?' we ask ourselves. 'I bite my nails. I lose my temper. I get into moods.'

Guess what. They do too. We all do.

When we're in a new relationship we tend to show our best possible face to the beloved. In doing so we may feel we're fooling them into believing that we're someone that we're not'. How can that possibly be? Our best possible face is also *us*. We're not pretending. We *are* that person. It would just be better if we were that person a bit more often.

In valuing the good in us, as opposed to concentrating on the bad, in loving ourselves, we are much more able to accept love from others.

The more you love yourself, the more lovable you are and the more love you have to give out.

Actually, that person you feel you're not good enough for is getting the bargain of a lifetime.

Accepting your worth

We've all heard of people who, having won the lottery or been left a large sum of money, proceed to squander it in short order, and are as broke two years on as they ever were.

These are people who are so uncomfortable with the concept of wealth that they can't wait to get shot of it. They may not be aware of this on the surface. They may even feel desperate rather than relieved when the money is gone. But somewhere they carry with them a deep-rooted belief that they didn't deserve it.

The money may have been more of a bone of contention than a source of happiness. Greed and envy can quickly spring to the surface when a large sum is involved. Everyone suddenly wants a share. Friendships are shattered through envy. Families that have been close-knit in poverty can come unstuck under the influence of sudden wealth.

People who deal well with unexpected windfalls are usually those who use their money to benefit others as well as themselves – making ethical investments, donating to charities, using their new-found wealth to loving advantage, rather than frittering it away on 'things'.

Know your worth. Money always feels better if we earn it. Fair exchange is, as the old saying goes, no robbery. And yet some of us are so unsure of our value that we allow ourselves to be robbed blind. By ourselves and others.

If you constantly undercut yourself by working for less than you deserve or underestimate the cost of your services, you are benefiting no one. Because no one appreciates anything they get for nothing. You will end up feeling resentful and giving less than your best.

Accepting your worth will make you much more comfortable around the exchange mechanism of money. Knowing what your value is will make you more able to ask for a rise when you deserve it. Being secure in what you have to offer will allow you to state your expectations when asked what you want in the way of salary. Loving yourself makes it much easier to fix goods and services at a rate which gives you a decent return for your efforts and lets you enjoy a comfortable lifestyle – all without feeling guilty.

This keeps the cycle of abundance moving.

Accepting yourself

Self-acceptance has two faces. One is forgiveness. The other is a belief in your own abilities.

Forgive your mistakes, learn from them and resolve to do better next time. This is something that can't be repeated too often. Don't dwell on foibles or failures. There is a lesson to be learned from every disaster. If you learn it, you have turned defeat into victory. The only defeat is in using defeat as an excuse to give up.

Love yourself enough to believe that you are special. Accept the unique gifts that you were born with and make the very best use of them.

Don't envy others their particular talents. You can do naturally what many of them would have great difficulty in accomplishing. Our talents are all appropriate, all worthwhile. Judging yourself against others is putting yourself on a hiding to nothing and is a serious waste of time. If the pipes burst in the middle of the night, a skilled plumber is more welcome than a poet who can move the soul to tears.

We all occupy a special place in the world. Appreciating yourself for who you are acknowledges this. It allows you to love yourself unreservedly and encourages others to do the same.

A grateful attitude is worth more than wealth or fame. Ingratitude pushes your good away. If you are never satisfied with who you are or what you do, if you are constantly setting yourself impossible targets and castigating yourself when you don't reach them, then you will eventually run out of steam. What's the point of trying if you can never please yourself?

Loving yourself means not being a perfectionist. Set standards, sure. Do your best, certainly. But the problem with striving for perfection is that you are dooming yourself to disappointment nine times out of ten. This is not a percentage that leads to a contented life. In striving to be the best you can be you are giving yourself the chance to reverse the equation. If you can be pleased with your performance nine times out of ten, you'll be a much happier person.

Give yourself every chance to be pleased with yourself. Allow yourself the advantage of loving who you are and what you do. Loving yourself benefits everyone.

Loving others is easy when you love and accept yourself. The love that you give is open and uncomplicated by a need to trade off feelings and emotions.

There is no blackmail involved. 'If you do this then I'll do that' is not a good basis on which to form any kind of relationship.

Love should always be given freely, with no thought of return. Giving love generously to yourself is the best possible preparation for giving love generously to others.

LOVE FOR OTHERS

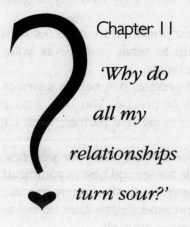

Chapter 11

'Why do all my relationships turn sour?'

Most people launch into romance as if it were a bad western. They shoot first and ask questions afterwards. With no inkling of what they want from a one-to-one relationship, they leave the whole thing to chance, hoping against hope that 'the right one will come along'. Or they grab the first person on offer, no matter how unsuitable, and then try to tailor their dreams to fit the actuality.

Instead of making themselves happy, they end up making two people miserable.

Does this sound like anyone you know?

Theoretically this is the rest of your life you're looking at. And, just as importantly, someone else's life. The least you can do is give your choice of companion as much thought as you would in deciding between the duck and the fish on an evening out.

Picking a permanent partner is like shopping for a new outfit. It's easier if you have some idea of what you're looking for before you start. Otherwise you may end up with an item that doesn't fit, doesn't suit your style or doesn't go with anything else in your wardrobe.

So the first priority is to make out a list of points which add up to what you see as your optimum choice of soul-mate.

Or, to be precise, you need a series of lists. And by all means *be* precise. You owe it to yourself as well as your prospective partner. Their happiness is also at stake.

At this point don't pull your punches. Don't be vague or settle for second best in your head. Describe the *perfect* lover. Be totally, utterly specific. You may have to compromise slightly later on but at least start at the top. Inspire yourself.

One proviso. Don't write down a particular icon such as Tom Cruise (or Demi Moore) and leave it at that. Tom Cruise is already spoken for (as is DM). And although you might think that Nicole Kidman (and Bruce Willis) have more than enough going for them, thank you very much, it's never good to take your pleasure at somebody else's expense – even in your dreams. What comes around, goes around and if you act like an emotional vampire you'll always be looking over your shoulder expecting someone else to do the same to you. Your dream lover can *look* like Tom Cruise (DM) or sound like Tom Cruise (DM) or even smell like Tom Cruise (DM). That's OK. But they can't *be* Tom Cruise (DM).

Anyway, where are you going to meet Tom Cruise or Demi Moore?

So perhaps you should prefix the list of your perfect partner's qualities with the following proviso – 'someone available'?

After that, of course, everybody's list will vary according to individual taste and personal preference. Just so's you remember the sky's the limit.

Now let's get down to basics.

List number 1:
Physical characteristics

How would you like your love to look? What *really* attracts you in a partner? We are talking wobbly knees and pounding hearts here. Remember no one but you need ever see the list so you can afford to be as honest as you like. Are you turned on by good teeth, neat buns, legs to die for? Go for it. There's nothing trivial or shallow or reprehensible about feeling a rush of adrenaline to the loins every time your mate walks into a room. You're short-changing yourself if you expect anything less.

Will your ideal be tall or short, fat or thin, blonde, brunette or redhead? Maybe you'd prefer no hair at all? Jean Luc Picard has just been voted the sexiest man on TV.

Next, consider what you *don't* like. Freckles, hairy chests, cheesy feet. Whatever – write those down too. Commit this list to memory. Why? Because you may be tempted to overlook one of these drawbacks in the first flush of hormonal excitement. If you do, believe me, it'll become a bone of contention further on down the line. Murphy's law states that bad points tend to magnify whereas good ones recede as an affair progresses. Whoever said 'familiarity breeds contempt' knew whereof they spoke.

List number 2: Character

Your lover's character should be of a type that would dovetail with, or at least complement, your own. Do you go for the strong, silent type, macho man or the life and soul of the party? Are you seduced by the idea of someone who makes you laugh? Are you attracted to power-brokers, ageing hippies, devil-may-care chancers?

Make sure you know what you're willing to put up with. Don't think you'll change your partner after the event. Not only does that *never* work, it's simply not fair. Would you like it if they tried to change you? The person you fall in love with is the person you fall in love with. Why would you *want* to change them? Yours is not to manipulate and nag. Yours is to decide what you want in the first place and then stick with it. Of such decisions are long-lasting and happy relationships comprised.

What *don't* you want? What if they snore, fart in bed, stay out with the boys, stay out with the girls, beat you, go crazy, have bad breath, drink the house-keeping money, invite their mother to move in? If you wouldn't find it acceptable under *any* circumstance, get it down on paper. You can always use it as the basis for a pre-marital contract later on. Why not? Would you buy a house or commit to a job without some guarantees? Choosing a permanent partner is a much more serious scenario than either one of those.

List number 3:
Type

Do you want someone with a career, a profession or a vocation? What yearly income would you prefer them to have (this more so that they fit into your own income bracket rather than that you can batten on to them like a leech). Would it matter to you if you were the major breadwinner in the house? Would it matter to you if they were? Would it matter to you if it mattered to them? Would it matter to you if it didn't?

Who wouldn't you marry even if they were dripping with gold? If you're a city dweller, uncomfortable living more than forty yards from the nearest disco or supermarket, a pig farmer from wildest Wiltshire might not be the best or more sensible option. You get the idea?

List number 4:
Interests

Again it's probably best if there's a point of contact here (the couple that plays together, stays together), although if you like a good deal of your own space, a golfer or a fishing fanatic will at least ensure you get the weekends to yourself. Think laterally. But *think*. James Thurber tells of one couple who split up because she liked Greta Garbo and he liked Donald Duck. The silliest things are important if you're going to spend the next thirty-plus years of your life with someone.

What would be a total turn-off for you? Someone with two left feet who thinks dancing is for sissies?

Someone with twinkling toes whose every available moment is spent sewing sequins on to a ball-gown? A rabid rambler, an iron-pumper, a football fanatic? You've no idea what a row-starter it is if, six years into the relationship, one of you wants to watch *Casablanca* and the Saturday night telly is permanently booked for *Match of the Day*.

List number 5:
Toys and tastes

Very important, this. Would you, for instance, feel comfortable stepping out in a Reliant Robin? Could you live with a matched pair of bull mastiffs? Might those five hundred Country and Western CDs clash ever so slightly with your eclectic jazz collection? Or would you prefer an Aston Martin (who wouldn't?), a Pyrenean mountain dog and a man who digs Count Basie?

These are not shallow considerations if you're sharing four walls.

The final step is to look through all your lists and pick out five or six main positive points – blonde, lawyer, wonderful legs, likes to travel, kind to animals, doesn't mind doing the ironing – that sort of thing.

This will give you an overall impression of your dream partner. It should also give you some idea of where you're likely to find them (at the hairdresser's, in the Inns of Court, on the beach, down the garage, at the vet's).

If you're looking for a foodie, how about enrolling in a Cordon Bleu cookery course? If you love the lambada, join a salsa class. If you go for artists, offer yourself as a model. If you're into Hell's Angels, leather up and head for the nearest drag-racing circuit.

All this focusing narrows the field considerably and raises the odds that when you do meet Mr/Ms Right, they're exactly that and not just a hopeful stab in the dark. You are no longer wasting your time 'advertising the world'. You've targeted your market.

If this planning sounds coldblooded, it's not. It's just common sense. If you're one of those incurable romantics who imagine that love has nothing to do with common sense, then think of it as insurance or, at least, stacking the deck in your favour.

Don't just leave your future to wishful thinking and random chance.

Once you've made your choice, here are some practical suggestions on how to push the business on.

- Relax. Nothing drives a prospective suitor away faster than a look of desperation. Enter any situation as yourself. Someone who is fine as they are. Open to offers. Free to make choices. Wanting but not needing to make contact. Be friendly to everyone. They may not be 'the one' but somewhere along the line they may introduce you to a cousin who is.

- Accept all invitations – to parties, open days, first nights, picnics, art exhibitions. While it's true that you could just as easily meet the love of your life in the queue at the post office, you increase your options by getting out and about as much as possible.

- If you live in a big city where it's hard to make contact, go out anyway – to galleries, the park, on river trips, down the pub. Be brave. Start conversations. It gets easier with practice. Work on your people skills. Sitting at home waiting for the phone to ring is not only a recipe for disaster, it's a sure-fire road to depression and self-doubt. Keep your social acumen oiled. Then, when a invitation *does* come your way, you won't have to start from scratch.

- Join in. Get involved with a political party, an environmental cause, a charity – local or global. Discovering how bad some other people have it will help you realize just how much love you already have in your life. Give some back. Practise caring. Help others while you're help- ing yourself to new friends (and possible part- ners). Give love out – on all levels – if you want to get it back.

- Pursue interests. Join a drama society if you're arty, the local badminton club if you're sporty. Do these things for the enjoyment rather than the romantic end. If you meet someone special consider that the icing on the cake. Whatever your talent, if you can play a good game of tennis or a clever hand of bridge, you'll never be lonely.

- Stack the odds in your favour. Get together with three friends, each of you to bring a platonic mate unknown to the others. Eat out, somewhere cheap and cheerful and non- threatening. Someone may click with someone else's sibling/old school friend/next-door neighbour. It could be you.

- Count your blessings. There are degrees of love – from all-consuming passion to the momentary glow brought on by a warm hug. Working from that perspective ask yourself who do you love and who loves you. Write them all down – everyone from your mother to the gerbil. You'll be amazed at how long the list is. If it's not as long as you'd like, provided you follow the advice in this book, by the time you get to the end it'll be twice as long . . . and growing. Put my name down there for starters. And you thought nobody loved you!

- Be daring. If you see someone you like, at a party, a club, the supermarket, ask to be intro-duced or, if there's no one around to do the needful – introduce yourself. Lurking behind the lettuces or lusting into your lager will get you nowhere. Speak up.

- Have faith. Like the proverbial silver bullet that has your name on it, if there's someone special out there for you (and there undoubtedly is) divine providence will make sure you meet somehow or other. Be open to possibilities. Who knows, you may even live happily ever after.

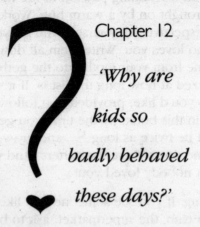

Chapter 12

'Why are kids so badly behaved these days?'

Kids haven't changed. They're you, before you grew up. You've just forgotten what it feels like to want what you want when you want it, to chafe under unwelcome authority, to have virtually no control over your life.

It's not easy being a kid. Try to remember that if you have to deal with children.

What do you do with a new baby crying in the night when it fell asleep only ten minutes ago and you can hardly keep your eyes open?

What does the damn thing want?

It can't tell you and you don't know one end of a baby from the other – except that both overflow with alarming regularity.

You wish the crying would go away. You wish someone would take over. But there is no one to take over. This is your responsibility. You're stuck with it.

And if they're older, no cupboard will be safe, no ornament sacred. Children have the most amazing imagination. They do things you would never dream of. They eat eggshells out of the dustbin. They spread boot polish on the Wilton. They get into make-up bags and draw on the wall with lipstick. Not because they're wicked, but because they want to know. What do eggshells taste like? Life is a glorious adventure and they don't want to miss a bit of it. They want to try everything.

Unfortunately, they don't know the rules.

It's our job to teach them the rules. Children don't come into this world fully equipped with table manners and social skills. They are savages. They need to be civilized. If you haven't the time or the patience to educate them they will turn into brats. That is, if they don't emulate the cat and kill themselves with curiosity first.

There will be times when you need all the love and self-control you can muster to stop yourself doing the deed in person. Children can stretch you to breaking point.

Some people don't have the love or the self-control to cope. The papers are full of such sad cases every day. Children abandoned, rejected, beaten and abused.

The myth of perpetual abuse

So what kind of unquiet spirit takes out its frustrations on a defenceless child? Children are totally trusting. Surely to betray that trust is the most heinous of crimes?

Theorists claim that victims of abusive parents, lacking a caring role model, react in the only way they know how when they produce children of their own. With violence. It's like a vicious circle which rolls relentlessly on through the generations.

But for every abuser there is an abusee who succeeds in breaking the mould. Determined that their child's experience will be the opposite of their own, some of the worst victims of abuse make the very best of parents.

It's all to do with perspective.

The copycat abusers are acting out of a lack of love. They never got it, goes their argument, so why should they show it? Now it's their turn to give back some of the pain.

On the other hand, the abusee who breaks the mould has stumbled upon the universal truth that love is not something you take but something you give. And in that giving, you get all the love that you can handle in return.

Dealing with the younger generation always means giving first. You're older and, theoretically, wiser. Or at least you should be. It's your place to set the example. And be prepared to weather all the changes that a growing child's affections go through. As babies they will love you devotedly and unconditionally, then they will start to question, and finally they will rebel. As some wit once said, 'There are times when parenthood feels like nothing more than feeding the hand that bites you.'

It's in the rebellion that you'll be most tested. For loving is not about giving in. Often saying 'No' is the most loving thing you can do for a child. Just be prepared that they may hate you for it. At the time. But if you're patient, if you're firm, they'll thank you for it later. When they're old enough to see sense.

lieve that if you're grumpy, depressed or in a bad
mood you pick a fight. When they're not enough to
cope with...

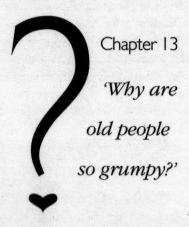

Chapter 13

'Why are old people so grumpy?'

The myth of the grumpy old person

The older generation suffers from an abominably bad press, most of it undeserved and out of date. The image of granny as a white-haired old crone sitting in the inglenook with her knitting still persists – in storybooks, in advertising, in the universal consciousness. Even though, in these days of optimum nutrition and early retirement, granny is much more likely to be hiking in the Himalayas, cruising down the Nile or learning to skydive.

So, if you were to take a random opinion poll of a cross-section of the population, the general impression would still be that older folk are bad-tempered, intolerant, boring, constantly moaning about the decline in standards and how much better things were in 'their young day'.

Admittedly some old people *do* become depressed and irascible. So might you if you were in pain, your body didn't work properly, most of the people you had something in common with were now consigned to the local cemetery and you had a rapidly shrinking future. But loads of older people are feisty and fun and full of the kind of wisdom from which all of us could benefit if we would only give them five minutes of our time.

It seems we no longer honour our ancestors. And whereas older people can look forward to a longer lifespan than ever before, with a large percentage now living into their nineties, the downside of the equation is that neglect and loneliness may mean that the extra time doesn't carry with it the quality of life that our senior citizens deserve.

Older people are notoriously overlooked in this frenetic modern world and, time being relative, there can be nothing as long as a long day in a nursing home with nothing to occupy the mind but memory and TV soaps and no one to talk to but the nurse who brings you your sleeping pill. In such situations many otherwise perfectly healthy old people give up and simply fade away. Imagine how devastating the loss of independence and identity must be for someone who has lived a long and fruitful life.

Older people ought not to be discarded like used tissues.

Superannuation will come to us all if we hang around long enough. As Doris Day so aptly said, 'The trouble with middle age is that you know you're going to grow out of it.'

The most valuable thing you can do for an ageing relative or friend is to allow them to keep their dignity and help them to retain their independence. If you are lucky, when your turn comes, there'll be somebody around to return the favour.

Almost all older people, even those who have lost a partner and are living alone, would rather stay in their own house with their prized possessions and their precious memories than be shunted into an old folks' facility or, worse, a geriatric ward. But the luxury of privacy is often overlaid with the spectre of isolation and neglect. So if you have an aged relative or neighbour who lives alone, try to make sure they are incorporated into the body of society rather than left out on the fringes.

Below are some ways in which you can offer your love and support to an older person.

- Include them in family treats whenever possible. Picnics. Outings. Trips. If they *want* to be included, of course. Some really old people find the energy of others overwhelming after five minutes.

- Offer to do any of those jobs which are now beyond them or which would cost a fortune if they got someone in.

- Encourage them to stay active. Take them out for walks (at their pace, not yours).

- Take them out to tea occasionally. It's nice to watch the world go by in convivial company, at any age.

- If you are cooking, make an extra portion and take it round.

- When you're in the supermarket, pick up an extra bag of potatoes or any other heavy item which they might find difficult to carry. Also bulk buys such as toilet rolls which are cheaper by the dozen.

- If their eyesight is failing, buy them some talking books or pop in occasionally to read to them (a short story won't take more than half an hour).

- Respect their privacy. Older people enjoy peace and quiet. Don't arrive unannounced. They might be having a nap. Phone first.

- Be careful not to patronize older people. And don't allow others such as carers or home helps to patronize them.

- Listen to the anecdotes, look at the scrapbooks. Even if you've seen or heard them many times before. This is a life. Many old people become garrulous in a bid to retain your interest. Like children they're afraid you're going to go away. Give them your attention and your ear and they'll become less agitated.

- Don't interfere where you're not wanted. Don't replace favourite armchairs or insist on re-arranging the furniture. Older people are less tolerant of change. It can confuse and disorien-tate them. The armchair is an old familiar friend. If they want to change it that's their prerogative.

- Many older people don't want to 'be a bother'. Encourage them to ask if they want anything. And be prepared to grant a favour if they do.

These are just some of the ways in which you can reassure an older person that they are loved and respected and not considered a waste of space. If you wish to implement any of them, be sure you do so from a position of affection rather than duty. If you feel you *have* to do something and don't want to, but you do it anyway, your offering will be tainted with resentment. Get the love bit right first and the rest will follow on naturally.

Something to think about

Picture an old dog, lying dozing by the fireside. You pass by, minding your own business. You don't even touch him. But suddenly he turns his head and snaps at your ankles. Why? Because he perceives danger. His faculties are no longer as sharp as they used to be. He doesn't see very well, or hear very well, or smell very well. When something looms too close, he bites, just to be on the safe side.

The next time an older person is less than gracious to you, or prejudges you unjustly, try to remember that old dog.

Older people are bombarded by the media with stories about muggers and burglars and venal children with the morals of alley cats. A small percentage of the most vulnerable *are* unfortunate victims of this vicious underclass. But a much bigger group are made to *feel* like victims for no logical reason other than that 'good news is no news'. They feel helpless in what they perceive to be an increasingly brutal and dangerous world.

Helplessness engenders fear and fear will produce bad temper.

Try to remember that. And give them the benefit of the doubt.

Chapter 14

*'Why can't
I get on
with my
parents?'*

The parent/child conundrum has spawned more theories, fuelled more therapists' careers, filled more talk-show line-ups, blighted more lives, than any other relationship in history.

Most of the problems arise out of a power struggle. It is hard for a parent to admit that 'their little girl' has grown up. It is even harder for us to shuck off the feeling that 'daddy knows best'. If these differences aren't resolved, if the balance of power isn't allowed to shift to allow us adult autonomy, then conflicts are bound to arise.

Parents remind you of a time when you had no power over what happened in your life. If they dealt with you harshly or unjustly, the feelings of fear and distress you felt back then may still be smouldering deep inside.

If you had a controlling mother or a father for whom whatever you did was never good enough, the resentment may well still be festering. A chance word or a thoughtless remark from them can unleash that resentment and evoke a wholly inappropriate response. Since parents are also past masters at making us feel guilty for our bad behaviour, when we react in this way we frequently feel ashamed. Blame and shame, the terrible twins.

Often the easiest way to deal with the situation is to avoid our parents altogether, to sever the ties and cut ourselves off. But even if we move to the other side of the world where we never have to see them, we won't have cleared up the anger.

The only way to do that is through forgiveness.

Forgiveness is one of the most healing aspects of love. It is also one of the hardest to come to terms with. But it's worth the effort. Forgiveness can clear away the dead wood of parental conflict and allow you to get on with your life.

Before you forgive your parents you first need to forgive yourself – for feeling the way you do about them. This allows you to release guilt. And when the guilt goes, the blame goes. Letting go of blame makes it easier for you to forgive them.

We are all quick to blame our parents for our own shortcomings. It is the easiest cop-out in the world. It means we don't have to take responsibility or do anything to change our behaviour. We can dump it all on them.

Forgiveness puts a new slant on things. If memories of past events are still screwing up your life then you need to accept your part in the process. Until you can do this you cannot truly claim to be an adult.

We all have power over our own thoughts. We are the only ones who can use that power to say 'enough'.

The past is over. That was then and this is now. Whatever happened in your childhood you can choose, if not to forget, then at least to see it in context – as part of the growing process. If you don't, then you will continue to allow your parents' will to dominate your future.

In forgiving your parents any real or imagined slights, in letting them off the hook, you reclaim power and responsibility. But to do this you need to be willing to *take* responsibility.

Decide that from now on, any time you start blaming your shyness on your mother's insistence that you should never show off, or your failure to land a job on the fact that the boss's resemblance to your overpowering father reduced you to jelly, you will stop, think and ask yourself: Can this person hurt me now? Physically? Here? In the present moment? Can they affect my life for ever? Or am I doing it to myself, in my head?

We all know of people who have risen above the most horrendous family circumstances and made a success of their lives. We also know of people who have allowed their past to grind them down to the point where they are unable to function in the present.

Their experiences may have been identical. The reaction to those experiences is what makes the difference. The winner uses pain as a spur to greatness. The loser uses it as an excuse to fail.

There is a definite choice here. The decision to be either a winner or a loser lies in your hands – not in the hands of your parents.

The good news is that parenting is getting better. Children are no longer thought of as chattels to be bartered or bought, sold into slavery or sent down the mines. Social attitudes have shifted. The Victorian father has become a thing of the past and mothers no longer leave a child to cry for fear that picking it up might spoil it.

The truth is that most parents love their offspring dearly, and do the very best they can for them.

Proof of the pudding is that more children are staying at home for longer and enjoying the experience. In fact some parents wonder when they'll ever get rid of them. More people get on extremely well with their parents than ever before, and look on them as friends rather than adversaries. Bringing the girlfriend home to meet mother is no longer a trial to be dreaded.

Of course some adults *have* been scarred by physical and mental abuse from which they feel they may never recover. This book is in no way qualified to deal with such extreme cases. There are experts out there who can. And because of the new attitude of openness, it is no longer necessary to suffer in silence or be ashamed of seeking help.

If nightmare memories are stunting your growth and holding back your development, there is more back-up out there than ever before. Take advantage of it to get back on track. At the back of this book are some options you might like to explore under *Therapy* and *Self-awareness Symposia*.

However, there are coping strategies that you can try at home.

- Compassionate detachment. This is one of the most effective ways of sloughing off the hurts, imagined or otherwise, of the parental past.

Whether we like it or not, we are all so close to our parents it is difficult to maintain a detached attitude towards them. In the beginning we look on them as God. In fact they *are* God, holding sway over our childhood universe, wielding supreme power, making the rules – and enforcing them – sometimes like the jealous God of the Israelites who was not above raining down fire and brimstone on the heads of his erring subjects.

Our disillusionment with our parents, and our blame of them, often stems from our realization that they are not omnipotent after all. They have feet of clay. It is hard to forgive someone you once worshipped for being all too human. We feel we have been the victim of a very cruel con trick.

Absenting yourself from this disappointment can lift a great weight off your shoulders (and theirs!). By detaching yourself from the hurt, standing back and viewing it as an outsider would, you can get it more into perspective. Aim to see your parents, not as blood relatives, but as individual human beings. Look on them from a position 'once removed', as it were. If your father were your best friend's father, would you still be embarrassed if he insisted on singing at parties, or would you find the whole thing funny, entertaining even? By allowing your parents their life, their mistakes, their idiosyncrasies, by acknowledging that they were doing the best they could given their knowledge and experience at the time they were bringing you up, you free *yourself* to move on.

- Awareness. Parents are not omnipotent. It only seems like that when you're three years old. It's time to redress the balance. Bring things up to date. Realize that, now you are an adult, parents and their opinions need have no power over the way you live your life. You no longer require daddy's approval for what you wear. You need no longer allow your mother to make you feel guilty because you didn't phone.

- Lateral thinking. Don't make assumptions. Maybe she couldn't care less whether you phone or not? Maybe she's glad to be rid of you! Were you so perfect as a child? Might it be possible, just possible, that you gave them as hard a time as they gave you?

- Defusing the situation. If a parent attempts to interfere or disapproves of some choice that you're making or tries to undermine your confidence, don't fume inwardly or lose your temper. Instead, remind them (gently) that you are no longer three years old. Thank them for their concern but be firm in your refusal to be intimidated.

- Role reversal. One of the most effective ways to cut the umbilical cord once and for all is to think of your parents as small children who need your love and protection. Try it. What kind of parenting did *they* have to put up with? Imagine your dad as a little boy being bullied in the playground, or your mother being laughed at because her family didn't have enough money to buy school dinners. You'll be astonished at how much compassion wells up in you. You'll be amazed to discover that you love them after all. You may even be able to forgive them.

- Clarity. Your parents weren't put on this earth with the sole purpose of embarrassing you or making your life a misery. They love you the best way they know how. They have done their job in teaching you the lessons you needed to learn in order to survive and to grow. Now it's your turn. Take the ball and run with it. Don't look back. Look ahead.

And here is a final thought. Suspend your disbelief for a moment and ask yourself, is it possible that you chose your parents rather than the other way around? Perhaps they were exactly the right people to teach you the lessons that you need to learn in this particular lifetime? If this idea triggers a long-forgotten memory – as it did with me – then see if you can work out what those lessons were, and whether or not you've learned them yet.

In the end, the best way to survive parents is simply to love them. The way you did when you were a child, before they hurt you or let you down.

They didn't change. You did. You expected more of them than they were able to give, even if they gave you all they had. You expected them to be perfect.

The connection is still there, no matter how far you may have drifted apart. It's up to you to stitch the wound, mend the fences, acknowledge your debt.

Not because you owe them, but because you want to.

Reach out a hand. You'll be amazed at how eager they are to grasp it. Pick up the phone. Write a letter. Tell them you love them.

Don't put it off. Parents don't live for ever and it's no good trying to clear up unfinished business after they've gone.

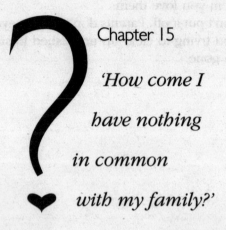

Chapter 15

'How come I

have nothing

in common

with my family?'

In days of old when the transport system was non-existent, people rarely moved from their home village. Everyone knew (and was probably related to) every-one else. Divorce was unheard of. There was no need of a social security system. The extended family provided.

Nowadays, relatives tend to be scattered to the four winds and only come together (if at all) at wed-dings and funerals. People change partners with frightening regularity. Older people are shucked off like so much baggage, as the faceless state's responsibility. This isolation of 'the nuclear family' of hus-band, wife and two point four children doesn't serve us. It is a waste of valuable human resources. It is a waste of available and unused affection.

How much better the Mediterranean system where you still see vast gaggles of family, all generations from great-granny to the tiniest toddler, gathered together in the local restaurant for Sunday lunch. It is a weekly celebration of all things enjoyable. Food, conviviality, conversation, the continuity of the generations. The meals last most of the afternoon. Talk is loud and continuous. A reaffirmation of togetherness in the common ground of shared genes. Deals are done, news caught up with and grandparents can view the results of their life's work from a position of warm respect rather than cold memory. Love spills over into the room, warming the surrounding tables.

A close family is a bulwark against the frailty of old age, the insecurity of the workplace and the degradation of cardboard city. If you have a family, extended or otherwise, treasure it. Celebrate its rights of passage: anniversaries and birthdays, passed exams and new arrivals. Any excuse to cement the connection.

Be grateful and be glad that you have roots. Some people are not so fortunate.

Ways to resurrect your family feeling

- If you have a sibling with whom you have fallen out, kiss and make up. You'll both feel better for it and it'll make your mother very happy.

- Call your mother and tell her the good news. While you're at it ask her to make you a list of known relatives back to her grandmother's time. Maybe she has an old address book? Certainly she will have some stories about family members told to her by *her* mother when she was a child. Note them down. Ditto your father. See if they have any old photos hidden in drawers in the attic. A mere two generations back (before the pill) families tended to be much bigger. You'll be surprised at how many relatives you actually have.

- Trace your history even further back. See whether an older member has a family bible with the names of your ancestors in it. Consult the local church records for births, marriages and deaths. See *Genealogy* at the back of the book. Check the gravestones in the churchyard.

- Construct your family tree. Get a book on genealogy out of the library if you're not sure where to start. Make it a project you do with your kids. Researching past lives can be a fascinating pastime. It draws people together in a common bond and can open your life out in all directions. Not only backwards in time but outwards to the four corners of the earth.

- Get in touch. Vast numbers of people migrated from Europe to the New World during the last two centuries, driven by war, pestilence and famine to seek a new life. You may find, as I did, that you have relations in the colonies. Look them up. They'll be delighted to hear from you. You are a link with their past. And pioneer stock tend to be much more open-handed and welcoming than we are. How great to have a cousin to visit in America's Deep South or New Zealand's Bay of Islands.

- Ask the oldest member of the family whether you can get their memories down on tape before they disappear into the ether. You can do this for your own amazement or fashion it into a radio talk or a human interest piece to offer to the local paper, *Reader's Digest* or *Choice* magazine (with the subject's permission of course).

- Write a fully fledged family saga. Turn your history into a best-selling novel, sell the film rights and retire to the Bahamas. Or at least, why not write it down for posterity? Do it in the form of a journal with relevant photographs. Keep scrapbooks with newspaper clippings and copies of diplomas or medals won. Fill in the details. Write what your feelings were, how things smelled and tasted, what the weather was like. Believe it or not, your trip to Torremolinos will make fascinating reading to someone in the twenty-second century.

So what has all this to do with love, and with caring in particular? A lot.

In making up with the sister you fell out with twenty years ago you are mending a family fence.

In connecting with far-flung relatives, you are proving to yourself that you are not an insignificant dot on the planet but part of a greater whole.

In contacting the distant relatives, you are doing them the same service, emphasizing their place in the world.

In rediscovering your ancestors' story you are allowing their voices to echo down the ages, bequeathing them a belated kind of immortality.

In recording your own story you are leaving a loving legacy for your children and your children's children. Through you, future generations will be able to plug into a folk memory of what it meant to live in this fleeting moment of time. You will be passing on a feeling of continuity in what may, by then, be an even more unstable and discontinuous world than ours.

Chapter 16

'Why don't I have any friends?'

Maybe you are again trying to get before you give?

We all want to belong. We all need to have friends; to matter to others; to enjoy company; to hang out; to be part of a mutually exclusive group.

But as with any relationship which involves caring (and it's hard to think of a successful one that doesn't), the most important thing about friendship is the holding out of the hand. If you are a friendly person, if you give off friendly vibes, then you will always have friends around you. If you are prickly and selfish and judgemental, you won't.

A true friend will stick with you through thick and thin, offer shelter from life's storms and a shoulder to cry on when things become too much to bear. So why is it that we so often neglect our friendships, to the point where some of them just fade away?

Time constraints? Change of interests? A new lover? Relocation? The reasons are many – the excuses few. But one thing's certain, friendship, like anything else worthwhile, needs nurturing. If you never cleaned your shoes, dusted your furniture or washed your car, you'd expect them to look pretty tatty. Friendships need the same kind of regular routine maintenance.

Keeping friendship alive

Express your feelings at every available opportunity. People love to know that they're appreciated. Praise. Hug. Tell people how much they mean to you. Never take the gift of friendship for granted.

Conversely, bite your tongue before you say anything spiteful in the heat of the moment that you will regret later. A second's unbridled anger can damage a friendship that has taken years to construct.

Remember birthdays, with a phone call, a card, a small gift. This may seem obvious but it's surprising how easy it is to forget and how miffed people are if you do.

I have a friend, Moira, who, like the elephant, *never* forgets. Wherever she is in the world (and at the moment she's in Sugarland in Texas), her friends invariably get a card (an appropriate one too, not just any old card) and a present (always beautifully wrapped). Moira is one of the busiest people I know. I used to think she was some kind of miracle worker until I discovered her secret. True, she has unflagging energy, but she's also wonderfully well organized. And she cares enough to make the effort. On her study wall she has an enormous chart with all her family and friends' and colleagues' birthdays marked on it in coloured stickers. Pink for family, green for friends, yellow for colleagues. It's not that she never forgets, she's worked out a system so that she always remembers.

Never underestimate the glow that remembrance brings, or the disappointment that people (especially children) feel when they're overlooked.

Make regular phone calls to friends who live close by. Always return calls on your answerphone as soon as possible. As you would for business calls. For friends further afield, an occasional letter or card (or a clipping out of a magazine that you think will amuse) keep the contact going.

If the 'friends' section in your Filofax is bursting at the seams (lucky you) and you are utterly fazed by the last two suggestions, make a list and work your way through it. One call or letter a week shouldn't be beyond even the busiest of bods (think of Moira!) and over a six-month period even the most popular person should have covered the bare essentials of friendship maintenance. Otherwise, suddenly, three years will have gone by, the person will have moved on and you may never hear from them again.

Arrange the occasional lunch with the girls (or boys). Whether it's a drink and a sandwich at the pub or the full works down the local bistro, keeping in touch doesn't have to be a chore. If it feels like it then the people involved probably aren't real friends after all.

Take holidays together. An extension of the above. A holiday with friends can give you a break from routine (and from the kids if you have them, provided you can get someone to take them off your hands for a weekend) or save the single supplement if you are normally a solitary traveller.

If you are going *en famille*, make sure beforehand that you and your friends' kids get on as well as you do. I've known the two sets of offspring of the firmest friends loathe each other on sight. Their bickering not only ruined the holiday, it opened a rift in a long-standing relationship that has never been healed.

Some friendships glow like a beacon down the years, others gutter and fade at the first signs of strain. Soulmates weather all kinds of adversity. Fair-weather friends disappear at the merest hint of trouble.

Here's how to tell the difference.

A true friend	A fair-weather friend
• Never takes friendship for granted.	Assumes you'll always rush round at the drop of a hat no matter how awkward or inconvenient it is.
• Remembers your birthday.	Forgets your birthday.
• Forgets your age.	Remembers your age.
• Won't take advantage (i.e. dump the cat or the kids on you at a moment's notice but always be too busy to return the favour).	Only invites you to dinner to make up numbers because someone else has dropped out at the last minute.

A true friend	A fair-weather friend
• Doesn't take umbrage if you don't phone for a while.	Drops you as soon as they move up in the world.
• Offers to help without being asked.	Never offers to help.
• Helps.	Never helps.
• Has seen you at your worst – drunk, sick, unpleasant, angry – and still loves you.	Disappears into the woodwork if you lose your shirt, your lover or your reputation.
• Doesn't gossip behind your back.	Reveals your deepest, darkest secrets to anyone who will listen and adds some extra just for fun.
• Wouldn't dream of chatting up your other half.	Seduces your partner.
• Celebrates your success.	Envies your success.
• Commiserates about your failures.	Couldn't care less about your failures.
• Listens to your problems.	Talks continually about their own problems.
• Never lets you down.	Always lets you down.

Reading through those two lists you probably found yourself nodding wisely at the first, tutting knowingly at the second. But ten to one you will have reviewed them only from the perspective of how you expect your friends to behave.

Time now to go back over them and see how *you* measure up as a friend. How many plus points do you score? How many minuses? Be honest. Given the choice, would you want you as a buddy?

When I was at school I had two 'best friends', Rosemary and Sandra. We went everywhere together, were virtually inseparable. Then, one day, a cousin of one of them moved into the area and joined, not only the school, but our cosy little trio. I took an instant dislike to her. To me, three was company, four a crowd. Poor girl, she never did anything to me to deserve it but I did everything I could to undermine her standing. Nothing worked. I sulked. I huffed. Eventually I issued an ultimatum: 'Either she goes, or I go.'

I went. And they let me. And quite right too.

As my mother would have said, I 'cut off my nose to spite my face'. I also learned a long, hard lesson. I spent the next three years alone – worse than alone, tagging along with people who didn't want me and with whom I had nothing in common.

We eventually made it up, we three, but not until the cousin graduated. And, if I'm scrupulously honest, things were never quite the same again.

Those three years in the wilderness, excluded from the warmth and closeness of like minds, taught me how precious friends are. Also *what* they are. And what they're not. You don't have exclusive ownership on friends. They don't owe you the pleasure of their company. Friendship is a privilege, not a right. Grasping and meanness and that green-eyed hyena, jealously, have no place in the equation.

Nor does one-upmanship.

If you think that friends should always make the first move (as in 'Why should I call, she never rings me?') you've put the cart before the horse. You're playing social power games, and infantile ones at that. If you don't change your attitude you'll end up lonely.

Pick up the phone. What does it matter who rang last? Friendship isn't a trade-off.

Renewing friendships

Get out the old photograph albums. See if there are people you've lost contact with that you wish you hadn't.

If there are, try to track them down. Through an old address book (even if the address is out of date, the current owners of their house may have a new number), the telephone directory or your mother or theirs. If they were school friends and your mum still lives in the area, she'll probably be able to find them. If you know where their mum lived, see if she's still there. She's bound to know where they are.

Be prepared to be disappointed. You may have outgrown each other. On the other hand, you might find that the years peel away and it seems as though you met only yesterday.

Making new friends

If your address book is a little light, look back at Chapter 11. Many of the suggestions on how to find a partner are just as viable if you are looking for friends of either sex.

Anything which brings about that sense of shared experience is a wonderfully nourishing thing. For both the giver and the getter. Friends can bridge all sorts of social, racial, sexual and age barriers. Offer friendship with an open heart and an open mind and the returns will enrich your life beyond measure.

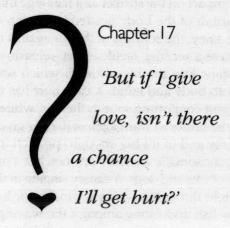

Chapter 17

'But if I give love, isn't there a chance I'll get hurt?'

Most people who withhold love do so out of a sense of fear. Fear of rejection or ridicule. Having a pet allows you to practise love free from that fear. A pet will lap up all the love you can give it. And once you experience the sheer pleasure of giving love for its own sake, it's much easier to allow it to flow into other areas of your life.

Recent research has shown that pet-owners, particularly those who live alone, suffer much less from stress than their pet-less counterparts. The company of another living thing, dumb or otherwise, apparently brings very positive results. The warmth of companionship, the need to take care of something, the unconditional love and gratitude received for that care – all these things give the pet-owner a sense of self-worth. Older people who have lost a spouse gain particular benefit from having a pet. This is not merely a frivolous fancy, it has a firm foundation in scientific fact.

The stroking of a dog or cat has the same physiological impact on the stroker as a massage might have. The warmth of the body nestled in the lap or alongside the knee, the softness of the fur against the skin – these have a sensual, tactile effect, releasing relaxing endorphins into the bloodstream which soothe and calm both body and mind. A cat's purr has to be one of the most comforting sounds there is, while having a dog in the house to warn against danger gives a sense of security and (if it's big enough) protection.

Psychosomatic benefits are not just confined to owners of cats and dogs. A canary singing in the stream of sunlight through a summer window or a beautiful rainbow fish undulating amongst the waving weed of an aquarium can bring a sense of well-being and tranquillity to a room. My dentist has installed a large circular fishtank full of golden carp in his waiting area. It's the ultimate in customer care – and a double plus for him, in that his patients come in for their treatment in a much less fraught state than if they'd been leafing nervously through a ten-year-old copy of the *Reader's Digest* for the previous fifteen minutes.

For companionship and undemanding love, there is nothing quite like a pet. For a moderate outlay and the basics of food and shelter they will give you devotion without demands. They don't care if you look like the back end of a bus in the morning and they never answer you back. To paraphrase William Butler Yeats, they love you 'for yourself alone, and not your yellow hair'. As for dogs, they are the ideal fitness trainers, ensuring that at least once a day (and especially before bed) you stretch your legs and get a bit of fresh air.

But owning a pet is a big responsibility. Having a living thing at your mercy is not something to be taken on lightly. Their welfare, their health, their very existence depends on you. Abandonment statistics are horrendous. If you feel you can't take on a pet, it's better by far to send a donation to the World Wildlife Fund or the RSPCA. Or you could always adopt an animal (see the back of the book for details). Some schemes have things like T-shirts and mugs and pencils which can have your pet's name inscribed on them. Or you can buy a picture of your pet to hang on your wall. These would also make wonderful presents for an animal-mad, city-dwelling friend or relative who can't have the real thing.

Inevitably, in the course of time pets die. If they have been a treasured companion for many years their passing can be as traumatic as losing a member of the family. Even a bird can leave a gap when its small heart stops beating. Are you ready for that? The easiest way to overcome the grief is to replace the pet straight away. This is no insult to their memory. On the contrary, it is proof that you enjoyed having them around so much that you want to repeat the experience.

Pets are wonderful company. If you are a single person they take the loneliness out of living alone. If you are at home most of the time, the little rituals of feeding and walking and grooming will give the day structure. If you are out working your socks off, coming home to a bird's song or a cat's miaow is much more comforting than entering an empty house.

But you don't have to *own* a pet or even adopt

one. Don't forget you can always put nuts out for the wild birds in the winter. You can pick up a pack for pennies at your local supermarket when you're doing the family shopping. The pleasure you get from watching the variety of plumage on display will be worth twice the price. While you're at it – and especially in frosty weather when the ponds may be frozen over – put out a saucer of water too. More birds die of thirst than hunger in the bleak midwinter.

Always remember that animals, whatever their size and shape, are living things. They are not there for your amusement or to perform tricks to impress your friends. If you take them into your home, they are your responsibility. They are not an ornament or an accessory. You must take them into your heart. If you do, and provided you give them the love and attention they deserve, they will reward you with hours of enjoyment, oodles of fun and the kind of uncomplicated devotion that will defrost even the coldest heart.

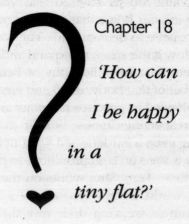

Chapter 18

'How can I be happy in a tiny flat?'

One of the best ways to give love to yourself and others is by creating a nurturing environment.

We've all been in homes where, the minute you enter the door, the warmth envelops you and the welcome reaches out in greeting. Comfort seems to be written into the walls, as indeed it is, because the essence of the owners is impregnated in the very brickwork. Some houses have been well loved and it shows. Just as certain others (where a crime has been committed or a family is in constant contention) give you the creeps.

A home does not need vast amounts of money spent on it to create a good atmosphere. Regular maintenance, clever choice of colour, lashings of love and a feel for balance and form are much more important. A minimalist Japanese room with clean lines, polished floors and one single perfect lily in a tall vase is much more pleasing to the eye (and the soul) than an indiscriminate clutter of paraphernalia hoarded to sustain a false sense of security.

Artist William Morris advised that you should 'have nothing in your home that you do not know to be useful or believe to be beautiful'. The spirit needs to breathe. Allow it the space to expand and develop.

The ancient Eastern philosophy of Feng Shui is based on the belief that body, mind and environment need to be balanced to produce harmony and happiness. No self-respecting Chinese builder would think of constructing even a garden shed without first making sure that it is sited on land propitious to prosperity and good fortune. Feng Shui works on the assumption that the world is criss-crossed by a series of magnetic channels weaving their way through the earth rather like the blue veins in a Gorgonzola cheese. These veins carry global energy (as the ley lines of the old Celtic religion were believed to do) and are known as Dragon Lines.

Feng Shui is gaining much more popularity in the West – as a kind of celestial home insurance. The domestic equivalent of acupuncture, it aims to release positive forces into the environment. Arranging furniture in the most harmonious conjunction, setting a mirror to reflect a particular view, placing a light in a relevant corner – all these are considered important, not just in the aesthetic sense but to create a channel to allow good vibrations to enter and occupy the building.

There is an old Irish belief that a bed placed north–south, so that the body is parallel to a line drawn through the Poles, will produce a better night's sleep than one angled cross-wise (east–west). I have always found this to be true. Of course it's all very well if your bedroom is of a size and shape to facilitate such a placement – not so easy if you sleep in one of those boxrooms where you would be hard put to it to swing a cat. But if you are a habitually bad sleeper, or have become an insomniac only since you moved into your new flat, it's something you might consider. And if you have a baby who is awake half the night, why not try turning the cot round?

If you are interested to delve deeper into the Feng Shui phenomenon, there are various books now on the market. Or you might hire a consultant to advise you, although at £200 or £400 a session they don't come cheap.

Alternatively, you could learn the skills for yourself. There is an address at the back of this book for details.

Whatever your lifestyle, here are some simple ways to give your home a welcoming atmosphere.

Light

Save strong lights for the kitchen or the stairs. Otherwise create ambience by adding pools of light with strategically placed lamps. Highlight a special painting or ornament, or use a floorball directed upwards through a plant to cast shadows on the walls. Angle a beam over your shoulder to illuminate a sewing or reading area, a desk-lamp to focus your concentration on your work. Mirrors placed opposite a window reflect light back into a dull room. Pink bulbs make a bedroom cosy and inviting. And candles. Candles everywhere. Singly or in clumps. Gone are the days when candles were kept under the stairs in case of a power cut. Now you can buy them in all shapes and sizes and colours, from tiny nightlights to giant columns of beeswax to floating flowers. Use them at the dinner table, in the bathroom, reflected in mirrors for double effect. Candles are mysterious, romantic, calming. They give the room (and your skin) a magical glow.

Sound

Less is more in the sound department. We are so besieged by noise these days we've almost forgotten how soothing silence can be. Try it. No TV, no tranny, no burbling DJ. It's in the eye of silence that great ideas materialize. Nurture yourself with a bit of peace and quiet for a change. Otherwise white sound is a good substitute. Wind-song, wind-bells, woodland noises, the swish of waves on a secluded beach. Classical music can be inspiring. Sit and listen to it, *really* listen, once in a while, rather than using it as an adjunct to the dusting. Pan pipes are intriguing. Pop music is a good, lively accompaniment to mindlessly repetitive tasks (like washing up), although it's very Zen to use such reflex actions as a moving meditation. 'Chop wood, draw water' is a Zen axiom, keeping the hands busy while leaving the mind free to contemplate the infinite.

Colour

Yellow walls will add warmth. Blue is the colour of tranquillity. Earth colours are relaxing, greens creative. Red is welcoming. The base colours of your rooms shouldn't shout at you, so keep them muted. Add bright touches with accessories – curtains, cushions, bed linen and lamps. Candles again. Bright bottles of bathsalts. Wicker baskets of coloured soaps. And flowers. Big bunches or single stems. If anyone in the family suffers from hay fever, substitute these with big bowls of fruit for a feeling of abundance.

Scent

Scent your home with candles or, for aromatic oils, use those little pottery scenters with the saucer in the top (to hold the oil) and the cave underneath (for the nightlight). The heat from the nightlight warms the oil which releases wonderful scented vapours into the room. Buy yourself a luscious selection, anything from heady musk to an exquisite ozone that fairly sings of the sea. Joss sticks are fun. Pot pourri is pretty and can be reinvigorated with scent once the original essence has evaporated. The trick with pot pourri is to keep it in a stoppered jar. This holds the fragrance in. Take the top off once a day for about half an hour to scent a room. And, of course, there is nothing quite as welcoming as the smell of home cooking. One friend who was having difficulty selling her home was advised by her perspicacious estate agent to have an apple pie in the oven when the next prospect came to view. It worked like a charm.

Contracts were exchanged within the week, even though the house had been on the market for nearly two years.

Fabric

Touch can have a soothing effect. Fill your home with smooth, luxurious fabrics – velvet cushions for your back, deep-pile rugs to curl your toes into, crisp cotton sheets under a duck-down duvet. Piles of big, soft towels (cut them up for dish-clothes when they get thin and scratchy) with full-length dressing-gowns to match. Crochet a bed-cover, make a patchwork quilt, cover the seat of a favourite chair with petit-point. Anything with love woven into it adds nurturing value to your home.

Memories

Relive the good times with photos in silver frames, collections (not necessarily expensive ones – stones, shells, matchbook covers or postcards can be much more evocative than standard tourist fare), books and paintings, CDs of your favourite songs.

De-cluttering

Remove anything which has become simply clutter. Have a garage sale or give it to the local charity shop. It may be beautiful in someone else's eye – there's no accounting for tastes. If it's broken and you're never going to get around to mending it, bin it.

Keeping cosy

Make sure your house is warm and draught-free.
Heavy curtains, loft insulation, double glazing – whatever it takes to make the place cosy. If you're short of
cash, buy rolls of spongy tape which you can fix
round ill-fitting doors to keep the wind out. All of the
above conserve energy and keep the heating bills
down.

Refuge

A home needs not only to be comfortable, it should
also feel secure. Unfortunately the days have long
gone when we could pop down to the shops without
locking up or leave windows wide open on the
ground floor on a hot summer night. You'll sleep
much easier if you have a professional locksmith cus-
tomize your home. You need deadlocks on downstairs
doors and ground-floor windows, and personalized
keys that can't be replicated unless you give the correct code number. Don't worry about the cost. You'll
easily recoup it from what you save in insurance pre-
miums. Incidentally, if, like me, you are an inveterate
key-forgetter, save yourself the embarrassment of having to call out the law to let you into your own house,
by locking the door on the inside when you come in.
If you can't get out, you'll have to find the keys, so
you can't forget them. Keep the keys on a hook near
the door. In case of fire you'll be able to put your
hand on them straight away.

A sense of place

Stamp your mark on your surroundings. More than anything, your home says who you are. And who you *really* are is not necessarily the face you present to the world. I know at least one woman, all efficiency and tailored suiting, whose name is awash with chintz and cherry blossom, and another, Laura Ashley to the life, whose apartment is all clean lines and high-tech chrome. If your house says, 'I am comfortable in these surroundings,' others will be comfortable there too. It's only when a house has the arid feel of being done up in the current style by a pretentious interior designer with money in mind that the sense of belonging is absent. And it is that sense of occupancy, of being at one with your living space, that makes the difference between a house and a home.

Open your living space to others

In Spain they have a saying: '*Mi casa es tu casa.*' It means 'My house is your house', and they mean it. The Celts, too, have a great tradition of hospitality, of making the stranger welcome. I remember my mother, on being invited to take tea at an English home, returning bristling with outrage that that was what she got. 'A cup of tea in my hand,' she sputtered, 'not even a scone.' Such behaviour would have been unheard of in Ireland, where sandwiches, soda bread and fairy cakes (and scones) would have been trotted out for the guest. This attitude goes back to the Bardic tradition of hearth and home – where the traveller brought excitement and entertainment to the dull routine of humdrum lives. The Bard was feted with the best the household had to offer, as long as he sang for his supper. You need not kill the fatted calf every time a friend drops by but a house that says welcome on the mat, and means it, will always be full of love and laughter.

Our homes are what we bring to them. The meanest hovel, provided it is cherished, is more precious than a castle that no one cares about. A house with love in it is rich indeed.

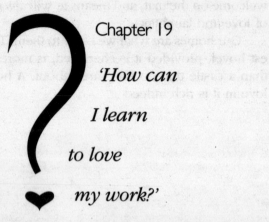

Chapter 19

'How can I learn to love my work?'

Giving your best efforts, whether you are a chambermaid or a brain surgeon, is what love in the workplace is all about. This is the idea of service.

Service is an ambivalent concept. In Victorian times it became synonymous with 'below stairs' and 'knowing one's place'. Being in service is often viewed as demeaning in these days of equality and self-actualization. But true service has nothing to do with tugging the forelock or being subservient. Being of service or offering a service of the highest standards and to the best of one's ability is something of which one can be justifiably proud. Especially since, by serving, you are showing your respect for the life of the person served.

It is not boring or square or naff to offer service.

Real service, not just lip-service. Service with a smile is even better. It is also good business.

No matter how clever or talented you are, or how brilliant your business plan, if you give grudgingly of the least you can get away with, if you mistrust your colleagues, pay your bills late and never go the extra mile to deliver the goods – in other words, if you work only for the money, you will never rise above the mediocre.

Latterly, there has been a move away from the 'greed is good' culture of the eighties. People have come to realize that quality of life is not measured by the things that one owns. More is not necessarily better. In the end, one can only live in one house, drive one car, eat one meal, wear one set of clothes at a time. In a world where so many have so little, conspicuous consumption is no longer socially acceptable.

A sea change has been occurring in the collective consciousness. Increasingly individuals are seeking happiness through the more spiritual pathways of self-respect, pride in achievement, closeness to family and friends, integrity and a sense of belonging.

Fewer people are prepared to work in a boring, repetitive or soul-destroying environment just so that they can trade in a perfectly adequate car for a bigger, flashier, newer model.

Some of us may feel we do not have a choice in the matter (though there's *always* a choice – it's just that we may not like the alternative). Still, if you are a victim of the 'golden handcuffs' syndrome, shackled to the mortgage and the school fees and the bills, you may think that there is nothing you can do but keep on keeping on. In this case, to quote Roosevelt, you can at least 'do the best you can, with what you've got, where you are'.

Whatever your situation, give it your best shot, to the ultimate of your ability, gifting the most rather than the least of what you have to offer – until you find something better. This honours you and serves those who pay your wages. If you are a clock-watcher, an idler, a skiver or an incorrigible absentee, you need to change your occupation, or your attitude.

Money is the currency in which we're paid to undertake the work we do. But money shouldn't be the main reason for doing the job. This doesn't mean that you should undervalue yourself or allow others to do so by paying you less than you're worth. Nor does it mean there's anything wrong with money. Often our attitude to it is at fault. It's as though we feel that in order to earn a financial return for our efforts we have to be doing something we dislike. Not so. It is perfectly possible to make money doing something you love. And here's the joke – if you love what you're doing, the satisfaction you gain is the major reward. The money is simply the icing.

Mind you, there are some jobs which are so stressful, so unsatisfying, that if you were paid a million pounds they still wouldn't be worth doing. Recognition of this fact is what accounts for the nineties phenomenon known as 'downshifting'.

This should not be confused with 'downsizing', which is where personnel are laid off to increase productivity – and the devil take the hindmost. But the two are inextricably linked.

Downsizing

Downsizing materialized during the economic depression that followed on from the boom years of the 1980s. Large companies (banks and privatized industries being the worst offenders) tried to improve their profit margins – for the benefit of their shareholders – by laying off employees in droves. A short-sighted and amoral policy, it took scant account of the human misery involved. This practice reached an apex of idiocy when one of the newly privatized rail companies laid off so many drivers that they had to cancel one-third of their trains because there weren't enough skilled personnel left to drive them.

Nor did this human misery stop at those made redundant. Those left in employment after the company, university or institution had been downsized frequently found themselves doing, not only their own job, but also those of their recently laid-off colleagues – often without any comparable increase in salary. This led to longer hours, more responsibility and greater stress in the workplace than ever before. It was a classic no-win situation. The companies concerned found themselves with a disgruntled workforce devoid of loyalty or motivation, who expended the least energy they could in order to get through the day. Productivity and standards suffered. More people were laid off. From this escalating spiral of discontent, the phenomenon of 'downshifting' was born.

Downshifting

Downshifting occurs when someone realizes that the game is no longer worth the candle. Having reached a threshold where they are unwilling to put up with any more, they decide to get out, regardless of the financial sacrifice involved.

Even those in the most powerful and highly paid jobs are having second thoughts. A mega-salary loses its charm when set against the stress, dissatisfaction, family disintegration, unsocial hours and impaired quality of life that one has to suffer to justify the big bucks. Increasingly people are choosing to question outmoded standards and trading a cut in wages for an upswing in job satisfaction. They are accepting a drop in lifestyle for a more rewarding existence, doing something they like and having time left over to enjoy a private life too.

Never think you're too old or too unintelligent to make a new start. Nowadays adult education is much more accessible than it used to be. In fact it's often easier to get into university when you're forty than it is when you're seventeen. Colleges are increasingly having to market themselves to ensure full rolls and therefore government funding.

Do the work you love and the money will come.

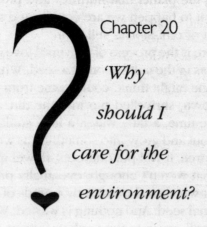

Chapter 20

'Why should I care for the environment?

The Native Americans honoured the Buffalo they were about to kill with dance and song, dedicating the soul of their 'brother' to the Great Spirit, giving thanks for the death that would sustain their life. The 'human beings', as they called themselves, were so at one with their surroundings that they believed the very stones to be fashioned out of the same essence as themselves (a theory now accepted by sub-atomic physics). They worshipped both wind and water and, like the Australian Aborigines, took only that which was needed from the environment to survive.

Today we cut down rainforests, de-nature the land with chemicals and pollute the seas that brought us into existence with our detritus. Farm subsidies and rampant bureaucracy result in huge butter and beef mountains going to waste while many in the third world die of starvation.

Don't think that we're not all responsible. Whether or not we take a pro-active part in the systematic stripping of the planet that nurtures and protects us, in *allowing* it to happen we are equally and severally liable. A sin of omission is still a sin.

Nowhere is the process of universal love in action so obvious as in the cultivation of a seed. What possible good, one might think, could come from pushing a small, brown, shrivelled pip into the dirt? And yet given a little time, a little water, a little sunlight, that pip will sprout and grow into something as wonderful as an apple tree. It will put out roots, flower in season and, as if that weren't enough, eventually produce a crop of fruit which will contain thousands of replicas of that original seed. And nothing is wasted. When the tree dies it will return to the earth to fertilize the next tree that grows. No assets are stripped, no lives despoiled to produce this miracle.

Love multiplies in equal ratio to that apple pip. A small amount, seeded where it is needed, multiplies manyfold. One of the simplest ways to put it to the test is to grow something for yourself. Experience the satisfaction of watching the miracle in action. Not only will it give you more respect for the process, it will also afford you enormous pleasure.

Why do you think gardening and cookery programmes attract the biggest ratings on television? Because both appeal to the nurturer in us. When we watch something grow – and then prepare it for our loved ones to eat – the mind, body and spirit are all satisfied.

Even if you live in a flat in the centre of town you

can enjoy the pleasure of growing things. Plants don't shout, wreck the furniture, come in drunk or run away from home. Value for money-wise they are hard to beat. A dash of water, a little sunlight and hey presto, visual delight. Colour (green is the colour of love), scent (if they're of the flowering variety) and constancy.

I have a monstera (you know, the one with the holes in the leaves?) which, if it wasn't draped around my bedroom window, would be ten foot high. It has survived two trips up and down to Scotland, the company of a couple of children, the hot summer of '76, various replantings and the disintegration of a marriage. It was bought as an eighteen-inch seedling from the corner greengrocer's in Belsize Lane in 1967. Now *that* is constancy.

Talk to your plants. The carbon dioxide in a human outbreath is like caviar to them. It nourishes them. So chat to your yucca, tell it how good it looks, use it as a sounding board for ideas, confide to it your deepest secrets. Plants don't tell.

Play them music. Recent research has shown that plants respond favourably to the classics and to white sound (wind, waves and woodland noise). If you find it soothing, they will too. And a de-stressed poinsettia, like a de-stressed person, can only flourish.

Also the water which evaporates from your plants will keep the air in your home from becoming too dry. Good for your wood, your leather sofas and your skin!

Outdoor plants will enhance any home. No one who has been to Andalucia could deny the visual delight of scarlet geraniums splashed against white-washed walls or showers of cerise bougainvillea spilling from balconies to bring a riot of intense colour to even the shadiest street.

Window-boxes not only brighten up a building on the outside; from inside they can be used to camouflage an uninspiring view. Planted cleverly, they can hold anything from snowdrops and crocuses to daffodils, primroses and pansies, one crop blooming as the previous one dies down.

Parsley, chives, mint and marjoram all grow well on the warmth of a windowsill. Begonias add glamour to a plain bedroom. Ferns flourish in the steamy heat of the bathroom and alleviate the starkness of plain tiles.

Decks, terraces and roofgardens are all urban possibilities. Built on slats of wood, covered in planters and creepers, they add an air of country living to the aridity of a town house, as do hanging baskets which can hide ugly pipes outside or in.

If you're lucky enough to have a garden, make the most of it. Rejoice in it. Nurture it. It's a gift to be treasured. Don't moan about the weeds or the fact that you seem to be forever mowing the lawn from May till September. What else would you be doing with your time? Watching *Coronation Street?* And please, please don't cover it over with concrete. That's urban vandalism at its worst.

At Findhorn in the far north of Scotland, further north even than the sub-arctic ridge of the Grampian mountains, the resident community has created a magical garden where tropical palms flourish and crops grow, not only in abundance, but to a much larger size and with a much fuller flavour than normal. People come from all over the world to view this phenomenon. How is it achieved? Not with chemical fertilizers, that's for sure. It's all done with love. Love is written into every part of the cultivation process. The planting is blessed, each seed focused upon as it is pressed into the soil. The young shoots are tended with devotion. And the gardeners sit among the bean-rows and meditate, passing on their wish that they should grow strong and healthy. Whether you view this with cynicism or ribaldry is of no consequence. The results are there for all to see. It seems that even the least sentient of earth's life forms respond positively to affection and attention.

Why don't you try it in your own garden. Do yoga there on clement days. Meditate among the marrows. Spread a little love like celestial fertilizer and watch the growing things around you sprout in sympathy. A recent survey has shown that palm trees, hugged daily, grow on average a foot a year higher than those that are left alone.

The Arabs had the right idea, turning their gardens into havens of tranquil symmetry with measured lawns, fruit trees for shade, rose arbours and crystal clear water. Their gardens were a source of peace and inspiration, where they could retire at the end of a long dusty day and contemplate the bounty of the world.

The Persian word for garden is Paradise.

If you don't have a garden and you fancy a bit of horticultural therapy, why not try to find an allotment? Begin by contacting your local council. You might just be lucky enough to live in an area where allotments are still rented out. If the local authority doesn't have a scheme and you know of council land lying fallow, suggest that they start one up again. One thing's for sure – if you don't ask, they won't offer.

Even without a garden you can still enjoy the wonder of the great outdoors. Join the Ramblers' Association or the National Trust. Contact your local tourist board about heritage trails. The best way to teach your kids respect for the land – taking home litter, closing gates, etc. – is by example. In Canada, which is probably the cleanest place I've ever visited, they have constant litter patrols combing the parks and gardens for rogue Coke cans. Even a heavily populated (and, it has to be said, extremely tacky) area like Niagara Falls is spotless. We've a long way to go in this country before we get to that point, but if we each did our bit and, more importantly, taught our offspring to do the same, we could get there. Litter is not the other person's problem. It's ours. So use the bins, take home your empties, carry a pooper scooper and never *ever* throw anything out of your car window.

Most people, given a pleasant environment, will respect it. Graffiti proliferates in soulless, concrete, urban areas created by short-sighted architects pitching the lowest bid, designing without human beings in mind. And not a bit of greenery in sight. Is it any wonder such places are vandalized? Who could possibly take pride in them? They are an offence to the eye and an insult to the spirit.

If we don't want to bequeath our grandchildren a science fiction nightmare, we need to honour the earth now. Your opinion matters. If you care, lobby your government through action groups such as Greenpeace – much more effective than voting for any political party. Nurture your immediate environment. It's part of you. Take a stand. Remember, you vote the council in. They are your servants, not the other way around. If you feel strongly about them cutting down the trees in your street, then state your case. Apathy will get you nowhere. Call the local press. Get together a petition. Don't let the paper-shufflers grind you down.

Some other suggestions . . .

- Recycle bottles/cans/paper.

- Use recycled paper whenever you can.

- Don't use coloured toilet roll. It may well match the towels but it also leaches nitrates into the water.

- Don't use kitchen towels. Buy bio-degradable cotton dishcloths instead. Washed regularly they should last for years.

- Get a shopping basket and take it to the super-market. Cut down on plastic bags. Give up cling film.

- Send a rude letter to the company that tells you you've been chosen to take part in their over-hyped draw. (What they want to do is persuade you to buy something you don't want in the first place.) Tell them to take your name off their mailing list. That kind of opportunistic marketing is responsible for the destruction of swathes of rainforest.

- Give up the car or, if this isn't feasible . . .

- Offer someone a ride.

- Join the Green Party.

- Support ecological activists. Whatever the media would have you think, most of these people really *believe* that the land is worth preserving. And they're willing to put their actions where their mouths are. They are much more responsible than those who want to drive yet another smoke-filled wedge through our countryside. They deserve respect rather than ridicule. Swampy rules, OK?

- Run for office. Become a councillor. And when you do, cut through the crap and get to the heart of the matter.

- Use your power to be heard. Make a difference.

Honour the planet and it will honour you. Always remember we don't inherit the earth from our fathers – we borrow it from our children.

LOVE FOR
LIFE

Chapter 21

'What is compassion anyway?'

Compassion, the final element of the love conundrum, is the most selfish and undoubtedly the hardest aspect to live up to. Love for its own sake. Pure love, with no obvious payback.

Frequently viewed as the prerogative of saints and martyrs, compassion is the silver thread which connects us to our higher centre. And it is from this centre that our own personal supply of love emanates. From there, it flows through us, outwards into the physical dimension which we know as reality.

The well of compassion is bottomless. It is self-renewing. But like the water in a well it cannot irrigate the landscape without our conscious assistance. We must draw it up and pour it out, bucketful by bucketful. Otherwise it will simply stagnate and go to waste.

Stagnation is what happens when we become

ego-orientated, grasping for our own selfish ends, clawing our way to whatever goal we feel will fulfil us, regardless of whom we hurt or step on in the process. We may reach our goal but we will still not feel fulfilled, because we have attained it at the expense of self-trust and inner peace. While we behave this way we will never be happy in our achievements, no matter how high we climb. Knowing how we came by them, judging our peers by our own nefarious standards, we hourly expect the consequent stab in the back. So we sacrifice contentment for a success we can never enjoy. This is the ultimate failure.

If you sow envy and spite and double dealing, that's what you can expect in return. Does this mean that it's impossible to be both successful and happy? Not at all. Happiness and success can be synonymous, provided the success is a result of honest effort and true merit and doesn't negate the rights of others to the same success. The answer lies in a compassionate attitude.

Compassion also connects us to our fellows. It allows us to see the world from other points of view. It lets us recognize the fear behind the ugly action, the pain that drives all evil. And it helps us to forgive. Forgiveness is salvation – for both the forgiver and the forgiven. It is a *very* scary ideal – because it's so hard to live up to. But it gets easier with practice. Compassion bridges the divide between self-absorption and self-awareness. Forgiveness connects us to the infinite supply of love that drives the universe.

Love as a spiritual force should not be confused with religion. Religions are made. Love simply is. And although most of the world's major religions claim to be grounded in love, on a great many occasions they lose something in the translation. What would Jesus Christ have made of the Spanish Inquisition? What of the holy wars currently raging round the globe? Not much compassion there.

These are human iniquities. We cannot blame them on God. The Maker who fashioned us also gave us the power to craft our own destiny. If we mess it up, we have no one to blame but ourselves.

Love may be part of religion but it is also a thing apart, available to all humanity, whatever their race, colour or creed.

Compassion is about love made manifest in our day-to-day living. It is about free will and choices and ultimately about survival.

Hate is also a powerful concept. A breeding ground for evil which fuels all the negative forces in the world. Anger and fear, dissatisfaction and despair, war and poverty, deprivation, degradation, famine, failure and pain. Hate destroys, tears down, obliterates.

Love, particularly compassionate love, lies at the root of all that is positive. Goodwill and charity, joy and abundance, fulfilment and well-being, courage and connection, bravery, hope, health, happiness and success. Compassion cements, builds up, resurrects.

If we embark on the route paved with envy and greed, we will experience misery and lack, whether or not we win the lottery. If we commit to the connected way then we can look forward to a contented, abundant life full of warmth and love. That doesn't mean we won't face challenges along the journey. It's through the overcoming of these challenges that we change and grow. It's in our reaction to the dragons that we meet on our travels that we prove our worth.

Life is a quest. Love is the magic thread that leads us safely through the obstacles to our heart's desire.

There really is a universal law of cause and effect. And it works for all of us.

The sword is a two-edged weapon, and if you live by it you can expect to die by it, whether you are an asset-stripper, a wife-beater or a war lord. As they say in show business, 'Be careful who you meet when you are on the way up, because you'll meet them again on the way down.'

Human justice may be blind. Cosmic justice never is. If you trample on those values which you know in your heart to be right, you may think you've got away with it, but you will get your come-uppance in the end.

Putting yourself on the side of the angels is never simple. One has to be constantly vigilant with oneself. It's so easy to choose the path of least resistance when things are not going well; to blame everyone else for our misfortunes; to pass the buck, when the solution lies in our own hands; to curse other people when it is our attitudes, our perceptions and our beliefs that are at fault. Awareness is sometimes a bitter pill to swallow. But once ingested, it can effect a miracle cure, bringing about a wonderful sense of freedom. It gives us back our control, rekindles our hope for the future. If we are responsible then we can do something about it. We are not pawns in some frightful game of chance. We can at least influence the outcome.

Compassion is the global aspect of loving. It involves not only those nearest and dearest to us but the whole shebang, heroes and villains alike. It is the umbilical cord which binds us to something bigger than mere self. A higher ideal. A greater good for a greater number.

And yet paradoxically, compassion must *start* with self. From the seed of selfdom it can blossom and grow into a tree large enough to shelter all-comers. Without compassion for ourselves, however, the seed will shrivel, the fruits wither on the vine.

Compassion for self is the starting point, the first step on the magic journey. It means recognizing your humanity, your frailty, your faults and your foibles without condemnation or self-loathing. It means admitting that you're not perfect. It means accepting yourself for who you are, rather than who you think you ought to be.

This doesn't give you licence to behave however you like and then say, 'Oh well, that's just me.'

The self has an infallible self-regulating button. You will instinctively know when you have done something you shouldn't and recognize that, in such actions, you hurt yourself as much, if not more, than the other people involved. Compassion for self permits you to forgive those natural falls from grace. It also encourages you to resolve to do better next time. From compassion comes relief and the strength to correct behaviour that ill serves either you or humanity.

Some people hate themselves. They are the ones who show the least compassion for others. They are the ones who deserve our compassion the most.

If you are one of those people then you need to learn to love yourself before you can love anyone else, or expect anyone else to love you.

Here are some ways to begin.

- Forgive yourself in advance. Realize that you

are doing the best you can, given the information you've got. You have always done that. So let go of past mistakes and move on. Now that you have more information you'll do better.

- Accept your good – a compliment, a gift, success – without guilt. Many people who are naturally very generous have great problems with acceptance. This is a form of selfishness, a controlling mechanism, a fear of being beholden or in someone's debt. Be gracious and say thank you. It's enough.

- Think of the pleasure you get from doing a good turn. Would you disallow others that pleasure? Permit people to do things for you for a change. No need to repay a kindness – simply pass it on.

- Reject unworthiness. Be your own best friend. You are a unique human being with a lot going for you. Remember the list of all your good points. Are you kind, generous, patient? Are you a good friend? A loving mother? Are you loyal, trustworthy, dependable? Commit it to paper. Bring your list out in the open where you can see it. Make a bookmark from it. Embellish it, colour it, cover it in hearts and flowers. Use it to keep your place in a favourite book. Every time you open that book you'll be reminding yourself that you are a valuable human being. Don't be so hard on yourself.

- Forget false modesty. Praise yourself. Appreciate your good points. If you do something well, acknowledge it with a small treat like a glass of wine or a walk in the park. If someone else praises you, be pleased, not embarrassed. Look in the mirror and congratulate yourself. Tell yourself, 'You did great. Well done!' Don't say, 'I could have done better' – otherwise where's the incentive?

- Don't apologize for being alive. Know that you are good enough just as you are.

- Acknowledge that you deserve the best. Everybody does. Ask the world for your good. Believe you can have it. Expect to get it.

- Try to be equally gracious in success or failure. If you win, don't gloat. Honour your adversary for his best efforts. Don't be envious or a sore loser. Learn the secrets of any defeat so that, armed with this information, you can rise to victory next time round.

- Never believe your own publicity. Know your true worth. There's a difference. The press has a way of erecting demi-gods for a day. This can give you a false sense of importance. The public is a fickle mistress. If you rely on the opinion of others to boost your ego, who will you have to run to if you fall from grace?

- Take criticism with an open mind and a pinch of salt. Be willing to see the truths and work on them. Constructive criticism can be an invaluable source of positive feedback. But recognize those people who are playing power games – trying to boost their own floundering ego and make themselves look good by making you look bad. They will succeed only if you let them. There's no need to resent them. Simply smile, acknowledge their comments and then dismiss them from your mind. Remember it's easy to be a critic and make sure you don't indulge in such power politics yourself.

The human condition is a frail one. We need all the love we can get. Love for ourselves, in the form of understanding and compassion, is a prerequisite for growth. Awareness of this will allow you to overcome any obstacle. Failure to acknowledge it will see you shying at every fence.

Compassion for self encourages you to see both your weaknesses and strengths dispassionately and, in doing so, make efforts to minimize the former and maximize the latter. It is the first stepping stone to a happy and fulfilling life.

Compassion for self will more easily allow you also to have compassion for those you come into contact with daily. To recognize that they have their problems as well. They too are doing the best they can. They need all the love you can offer. Give them all you have to spare.

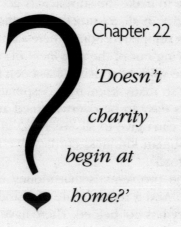

Chapter 22

'Doesn't charity begin at home?'

Charity is another word which, like service, has taken on unwelcome connotations. In its original meaning of compassionate goodwill, charity brought people together through generosity on the one hand and gratitude on the other. This has somehow been transmuted into a feeling of separation where the giver is elevated and the recipient debased. Acceptance of charity is now seen as something of which to be profoundly ashamed, while giving has been reduced to a gesture which promotes superiority or (when one is coerced into donating) resentment.

Drastic cuts in government funding have produced an overload of charities competing for our spare cash. In many cases up to 90 per cent of the monies collected by charities are spent on running costs and marketing rather than benefiting the people, places and things they were set up to support.

A vast number of us are 'all charitied out'. We give, not from a wellspring of generosity, but to salve our consciences or to make the supplicants go away. Often we don't give at all, tossing the begging letters in the rubbish bin unopened. Somewhere along the way, the idea of giving out of the goodness of our hearts, from a genuine spirit of concern, has been lost.

There are so many seemingly desperate cases in the world, it is easy to be overwhelmed and decide that, since we can't give to all, we won't give to any. The milk of human kindness curdles. We buy a lottery ticket instead.

One of the problems is that money is such an emotive issue. And a recent spate of scandals in the charity industry has not helped. There have been stories of directors fiddling the books, living high on the hog, employing their relatives in lucrative positions regardless of their qualifications for the job. And in one notorious case, it was revealed that one of the so-called homeless had been swanning around in a luxury flat when he wasn't driving his brand new BMW to the site where he daily sold *The Big Issue*, a publication aimed specifically at getting the dispossessed back on their feet.

These admittedly isolated cases are also the ones which attract the most press coverage. And since they are seldom counterbalanced by reports of the thousands upon thousands who give their time gladly, free of charge, to help those less fortunate than themselves, the public are left with the impression that all charities are corrupt, all homeless people on the fiddle, and all beggars crafty, work-shy malingerers.

Gifting money is valueless if you give grudgingly. The spirit in which you make your contribution is as important as the amount. Give with love or not at all. Otherwise your offering will be tainted. And if you have a problem with money then you need to address that before you pass any of it on.

If you think of cash as 'filthy lucre' that 'doesn't grow on trees', if you believe that there's never enough to go round, that it's the 'root of all evil' and that anyone who has enough and to spare must have come by it dishonestly, then you need to clear up those misconceptions before you do anything else. Living like Scrooge binds you to a reality governed by lack. Generosity of heart and purse opens the door to abundance, not only for those in receipt of your largesse but for you too. A good financial deed cast upon the waters of life will be returned to you with interest, whether in hard cash or in kind. Not that this is the reason why we should gift money. Gifting, like virtue, should be its own reward. It just so happens that good works inevitably attract unexpected perks.

Money is simply a form of energy – nothing more. It carries only the value we invest in it. Gold is precious because of perceived scarcity but money today is only pieces of paper with lines drawn on it. It has no intrinsic worth. It is valuable only for what it can buy us and how those acquisitions make us feel. Increasingly wealth is represented by a series of numbers on a video screen or a piece of plastic which we hand to the checkout girl to prove we can afford the groceries.

If your belief is that money is hard to come by, you will be less willing to part with any of it. It's only when you realize that there is plenty out there for everybody that you stop hoarding it. It is hoarding, like panic buying or runs on the bank in times of financial crisis, that causes scarcity and collapse. Keeping it in circulation means that everybody gets what they need – maybe not what they want, but what they need.

Currency, whether it be in cowrie shells or silver ingots, needs to keep moving to do the most good. If you spread it around it creates value for many people. The money you spend on a pound of potatoes at the supermarket goes to support not only the farmer who grows the product but the packers, the shelf-stackers, the hauliers, the salespeople, the advertising companies, the cleaners, the checkout girls, the boy who collects the trolleys from the car park. Viewed that way, every shopper is a philanthropist.

If you keep your money in a sock under the bed, not only will it not contribute to anyone's welfare (including yours), it will depreciate in value until the sock is worth more than what's in it.

The best way to deal with money is to get it out into the marketplace, to allow it to drive the wheels of commerce and promote the good of all concerned. Money can be a compassionate source of interconnection.

If you consider money this way, as a loving producer of abundance, it is much easier to gift some of it in a spirit of charity to those who are in need. And, like love, the more money you give out, the more of it you will attract.

Here are some suggestions to get your charity engine firing on all cylinders.

- Live in a grateful attitude. If you daily count the

things that you have going for you and all the wonderful abundance that surrounds you, you will realize that you have more than enough to spare.

- Respect the recipient of your generosity. Gift money as love – not blackmail. Charity is not about 'I give you this – you owe me that.' It's about 'I have plenty – please share with me.' Offered in such a spirit, the giving makes you feel richer, rather than poorer. It says you can afford it and still have some left over.

- Give with pleasure, to something you believe in. This can be your favourite charity, your church organ fund or to set up a trust for your talented godson's education. Each time you write a cheque, focus on the pleasure the money is going to generate. Think of the good it will do, the comfort it will offer, the knowledge it will promote, the faith it will serve, the beliefs it will bolster. This is money as light, piercing the darkness of ignorance and despair. Know you are making a difference.

- Tithing. This used to be standard practice in the Church. Less so these days where all that is left of it is the Sunday collection plate. The Mormons, though, still stick to the old way. They regularly tithe 10 per cent of all their earnings and that contribution is returned to them in educational standards and community stability. Clever business management has made Salt Lake City one of the wealthiest urban areas in the United States. Their Micro Library, the most comprehensive in the world, is a source not only of invaluable information to all-comers but of welcome revenue for the community. Each member of the Church of the Latter Day Saints receives well over and above the cost of their tithe in life-enhancement value. This is money well spent and a true example of loving financial energy multiplying to the benefit of all concerned.

And no, I am not a Mormon.

- Taxes and bills. Pay these with thanks rather than grumbling. Your taxes go towards shoring up the fabric of our civilization. Without taxes, schools and hospitals would be the prerogative of the rich and we would be driving to work along unlit, unpaved roads. As for the utility companies, they trust us to use the energy they generate for a full three months before they bill us. That energy keeps us warm, allows us to cook our food, take long, hot baths and watch TV. This is a privilege – not a right. Shouldn't we be grateful rather than resentful? Next time you write that cheque for the gas bill, remind yourself as you stick down the envelope how lucky you are to have such a source of supply and to be able to pay for it. You might even want to put a little X on the back before you send it on its way. SWALK.

- Lazy money. I make a point never to give money at Christmas or at birthdays – unless it is specifically requested. I know the excuse for sending a cheque is that you don't know what they want or, worse, you don't want to buy something they actively don't want. But a gift should carry a thought with it. We often use a hastily scribbled cheque as a way to get out of a trip to the shops or to release us from the bother of making an effort to choose something just right for the recipient. I call this 'lazy money'. With a gift the thought is more important than the amount spent. Here is an example. I love candles and, for Christmas past, my daughter, Sara, bought me a brass candle-snuffer. It can't have cost a great deal – she is married with two small children and money is tight – but she couldn't have chosen better. It's something I would never have thought of buying for myself yet I absolutely *love* it. Not merely because I use it every day but because she took the trouble to hunt it out for me with two infants in tow. I get a warm feeling every time I pick it up. And I pick it up often. Now *that's* what I call a present.

Another reason for not giving money as a substitute for a gift is that it has a tendency to get swallowed up in the housekeeping. I don't want a bottle of washing-up liquid for Christmas – do you?

- Beggars, buskers and *The Big Issue*. When should you give? This is a matter of personal preference and individual conscience. I always give to buskers and pavement artists, who brighten the day. And despite the adverse publicity, I still buy *The Big Issue*. You can't blame the whole barrel for one rotten apple. Also the people who sell it are learning the value of free enterprise (they get to keep half the proceeds of their sales). I never give to well-fed teenagers with hang-dog expressions and children on their knees who crouch at the bottom of the stairs in tube stations rattling tins. I consider setting such an example to a child to be iniquitous and I don't feel able-bodied professional beggars should be encouraged. You, of course, must make your own choices. If in doubt, listen to the feeling in your gut. Most people know instinctively when they're being conned.

- Consider the levels of abundance. If you're ever in doubt about how much you have, look around you if you go on holiday to a third world country. Please don't flash your money about – not because you might get it pinched but because your holiday spend could probably feed a family of six for a month and it's arrogant to rub it in. This is one reason why I never haggle. If I want something I pay the first asking price. It's all a matter of value and worth. My souvenir, their living.

- When NOT to gift. Do not give when your continuing support disempowers the recipient's growth. This applies to professional beggars and to offspring who, having left school, are too idle to get up in the morning because they know you'll feed them. Sometimes you have to be cruel to be kind.

- Become an ethical investor. If you play the stock market, use investment money to benefit the planet by putting your savings into companies that improve rather than destroy the quality of the environment. For advice on how to make a profit and a contribution at the same time, consult *The Ethical Investor*, a book by Russell Sparkes.

Money is so often the symbol that separates the haves from the have-nots. Unequal distribution gives rise to envy and jealousy, greed, resentment and apathy.

And yet, when used as a vehicle of compassion and contribution, money can become a force for good rather than evil, a source of hope as opposed to despair.

Spread a bit of it around. Make it a channel of connection in your life. Be charitable in the true sense of the word. And it can only bring you joy.

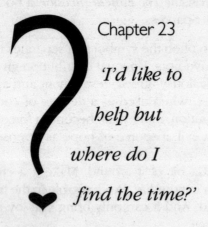

Chapter 23

'I'd like to help but where do I find the time?'

Time is the most precious gift you can give. Much more precious than money. Unlike money, you have no hope of ever getting it back. Time and love together make a priceless combination. Giving your time in a good cause is the true meaning of charitable compassion.

But time is a finite commodity, in this lifetime anyway. So before you give it away, you must first gift some to yourself.

These days we seem to have so little time to spare. Rushing from place to place, chasing our tails, trying to cram more and more into the same 24-hour span.

It's as if we're afraid to slow down. As though, if we do so, everything will grind to a halt. Of course it won't. The world will go on turning, the moon waxing and waning, the universe expanding, without our help.

If you are caught up in a frenzy of ceaseless, meaningless, repetitive activity then perhaps it's time you stepped on to the sidelines and asked yourself exactly what you're doing. You could be driving yourself to an early grave.

Take time to consider the pace at which you're living. Otherwise your allotted span may turn out to be a lot shorter than you'd like.

Grab a piece of paper and a pen. Not when you've finished reading the chapter. Now. Time is of the essence.

Ready? OK, now write down all the things you did yesterday. Even the unimportant things. *Especially* the unimportant things.

Divide that list into three mini-lists.

- Things you did for yourself.

- Things you did for other people.

- Things you needn't have done at all.

If lists two and three are longer than list one (and I'd lay odds that they will be), then you need to do a bit of re-balancing. Only when you have enough time for yourself can you afford to gift some to others. You should never be bottom of the heap or last in the queue. This is your life.

The reason for writing things down is that you can see at a glance where your time is going. Often we adopt a pattern of behaviour without even realizing it, or it creeps up on us gradually until we're careering around like headless chickens, going nowhere fast.

With the three lists in front of you, you no longer have the excuse of ignorance. And you can review what needs to be done. It's extraordinary how much time you can conjure out of thin air this way.

We're going to tackle each of the three lists in turn. In reverse order. Like the announcement of the winner of Miss World.

So start with List No. 3. Cross off *everything* which isn't essential. Quentin Crisp said of dusting that if you didn't do any, after three years it didn't get any worse. Dust once a week by all means, but every day is a waste of time. Delete all the trivia.

On to List No. 2. Again cross off everything that isn't directly to do with you. People have a habit of asking you to do something as a favour and then, when you've done it twice, consider it's their right. Don't let them. Your time is yours to give – if you so desire. It shouldn't be taken from you by force. Time theft is a crime. Delegate the 'favours' back to the muggers involved.

And so to List No. 1. If it's short on things like relaxation and fun, programme some in now from the time you've saved from the other two.

My guess is, you'll still have some left over to spend – voluntarily – on some deserving cause. Donate it with love.

Research has shown that people who get involved live longer, happier lives. Apparently the selfless gifting of time and energy floods the organism with good vibrations. Contributing to others' welfare also brings us face to face with our own good fortune. That grateful attitude again. And whereas donating money is a perfectly valid gesture, it lacks the hands-on approach of actually making a difference, in the here and now, to someone old or lonely or ill. A hand to hold is much more comforting than an anonymous donation, no matter how generous or well-meaning.

Often it's easier to be charitable to strangers than blood kin, especially if they're crotchety or ungrateful. If you have a relative who's old or infirm, make a point of letting them know they're not forgotten with a phone call. Remind yourself that a day in the life of someone bedridden or in pain can feel like a year. That way, the hour you spend with them on a Saturday afternoon won't seem too long or too wasted.

There are plenty of ways to gift your valuable time. You could become a hospital or prison visitor. Deliver meals on wheels. Read to the blind. If you're horsey, why not become involved with Riding for the Disabled? If you have a car, ferry disadvantaged kids on a day out to the country. If you have enough inner strength, help out in a hospice. Just being there for someone can help calm a frightened soul at a time of terminal crisis (see the end of the book).

With all of these things, commitment is as important as compassion. You will do more harm than good if you volunteer and then let down those who are relying on you. So make sure you know what you're letting yourself in for before you start.

Speaking of which, if you are considering offering crisis counselling with the Samaritans or Relate, ask yourself how strong you feel. How secure are you in yourself? This kind of volunteer work can be emotionally draining. If you're just coming out of your own crisis, perhaps it's not the best time to involve yourself in other people's problems? You will empathize but if you still need to scream, to project your own misery, you may reinforce rather than reassure. Allow the knowing and the recovery to sink to a deeper level. Then offer help. When the light shines at the end of your particular tunnel, you will be able to pass on the confidence that things *will* get better.

Perhaps you have practical skills? If you love to knit but there's no one to do it for any more, why not use your talent to create some warm woollies for sale in the charity shops or to send directly to the homeless or the war zones?

If you're a good cook you can donate food. The home-made cake stall is always the first to clear at any charity bazaar. And *everyone* is grateful for a handyman to do those little jobs like changing washers or even light bulbs – a major problem if you're old or disabled.

My dad, a retired headmaster in his eighties, learned late in life how to crochet, of all things. He does it while he's watching TV. It keeps his fingers supple and he says it makes him feel he's wasting less time than if he was just sitting in front of the box like a blob. He creates wonderful, colourful bedspreads, knee-rugs and cushion covers from old, un-picked jumpers which arrive at the Oxfam shop but are too tatty to sell. Recycled, they go like hot cakes. The activity and the admiration he receives for his efforts also make *him* feel useful.

Charity shops are great fun. Everybody loves a bargain. Sorting out those plastic bags is like going through a childhood lucky dip. It can also be an eye-opener. You'd be astonished what some people throw away. You'd also be astonished what some people feel is worth selling. If you're making a donation, please don't put in anything that ought to be relegated to the dustbin. Gifts should be clean, undamaged and reusable, otherwise why should anyone want to pay good money for them? If you're a lonely soul yourself, a couple of days working in the shop will get you back into circulation. You'll need to be willing and able to stack and rack, give correct change, know your stock and have a genuine interest in the customers. Charity work should always be undertaken in a spirit of goodwill, never as an exercise in superiority or self-importance. You won't be paid but you'll usually get expenses, so you shouldn't be out of pocket.

Charities are frequently desperate for funds, so if you've got the gift of the gab – either on the phone or in person – they'll welcome you with open arms. They always need people who can charm contributions out of business and industry. Otherwise you could run a garage sale, a jumble sale or a bring-and-buy stall for a good cause, or organize a sponsored event such as a fun-run or a swimathon or a baked-bean eating competition. These don't have to be at national level or raise astronomical amounts. Every little helps. A fete at the local church hall to send the Brownies to camp is just as valid as Children in Need, although your home-town event may act as a small piece in just such a larger jigsaw. These do's generate a wonderful sense of camaraderie and contribution – or at least they should. Try to keep committees to a minimum. They have a tendency to degenerate into petty power politics if you're not careful.

Christmas can be a very unhappy time for those not involved with family. All those pictures of cosy firesides with chestnuts roasting and songs about being 'home for Christmas' only serve to rub in the loneliness. As a charitable act you might consider inviting someone who's away from their nearest and dearest (or who doesn't have any) to spend Christmas Day in the bosom of your family. Contact your local college or university and see if there are any overseas students around who'll be on their own over the holiday period. People make so much food at Christmas dinner time you can always squeeze one more in. Similarly, you might make the remains of that turkey everybody's always complaining about having to 'eat up' into sandwiches and take them down to the nearest branch of cardboard city with a couple of flasks of hot coffee. You won't hear many complaints there. Or pay a visit to the hospital's geriatric ward and take a Christmas rose to the person who hasn't any visitors. There are so many lonely people out there who would be grateful for some of your time and attention.

Letters and postcards are a great way to keep in touch. Letter writing is now somewhat unfashionable, but unlike a phone call a letter can be enjoyed again and again. It can also be passed around or, if it's private, tied up in pink ribbon and read years hence to revive the memory of love gone by. And where would all those biographers of the rich and famous be without letters?

Got a little time on your hands? What, not even a measly five minutes? Why not use it to surprise someone with a phone call? Someone you haven't spoken to in a while. Go on – you know they'd love it.

And while you're busy, if you'll excuse me, I'll just give my mother a quick ring.

Chapter 24

'Why does nothing ever last?'

We all have a tendency to cling to attachments long after their emotional sell-by date. Lovers, children, lost youth, outgrown needs, outworn clothes, old beliefs, habits that no longer serve us. We hold on to them for grim death when often the kindest, most compassionate course for all concerned would be simply to let them go.

It takes tremendous courage to loosen the ties of familiarity. But in the end, it's less painful to go with the flow than to battle against the current. The one constant in this life is that nothing is static. Just as the year turns, so relationships, habits and ideas go through an inevitable process of alteration. We are either reinforced and tempered in this furnace of experience or we naturally burn out.

We are all shapechangers. Do you look the same as you did when you were three years old? Is there even one feature left that would connect you with a photo of your former self? Our skin, organs, physical selves are in a constant state of flux, shedding dead cells, sloughing away outworn tissue. Moment by moment we evolve.

Our minds and emotions also change. And sometimes they move away from the very things to which we once felt we were inextricably attached. This can cause a lot of grief and guilt and pain. Especially in relationships.

We all fear change. Even change for the better. Why else would unhappy partners stay in loveless marriages or women suffer years of physical abuse? Fear of the unknown can chain us to a present that has long outgrown its usefulness. Sometimes it's necessary to break those chains. Only then can we set ourselves free to address the future. When all other options have been explored and found wanting, we need to learn to let go so that we can move on.

Many who have been abandoned by lovers find it impossible to let go. The image of the beloved seems to haunt them, long after the physical presence has gone. Fixated by thoughts of the good times or obsessed by the bad, they endlessly replay the hurts, slights and the eventual break-up, living through the painful experience many times instead of just once. If you are conducting a post-mortem over a relationship that needs to be given a decent burial, it's time you allowed the hurt to rest in peace. For your own sake.

Ask yourself who is miserable here, the abandoner or the one left behind?

Which one has the power?

Which one is giving their power away?

Though we cannot control life, we can control our reaction to it. In order to reclaim the power of choice in such a situation, one must first give oneself permission to let the past go. To forgive and forget. Not for the sake of the deserter but for our own sake, so that we can clear the decks and make way for whatever new adventure life has in store.

The alternative is to end up like Charles Dickens's Miss Havisham, trapped in a decaying wedding dress, dying by inches in a darkened room.

If you are having difficulty letting go of a lost love, here are some strategies that might help.

- Acknowledge that, even if the end of the affair was painful, the beginning, and possibly the middle too, enriched your life at the time.

- Realize that, in forgiving, you don't need to condone or even understand the other person's behaviour. You release the hurt.

- Recognize that everyone has the right to move on. It is never easy to make a break of this kind. Would you have been any happier if your lover had stayed to make both of you miserable?

Free yourself up. Don't let bitterness and spite stop you from taking a future chance on love. Bitterness hurts the giver, not the receiver. And revenge is *never* sweet.

If, on the other hand, you are in a relationship which clearly no longer brings joy to either party and

you are desperate to leave, better by far to try to ne-
gotiate an amicable parting than wait for an inevitable
split. Couples who disengage voluntarily, allowing
each other the privilege of choice, tend to remain
friends. They are better able to work out a new form
of ongoing communication. A love affair that winds
down to a natural conclusion does much less emotional damage than one that has been bludgeoned to
death.

We are all individuals and, as such, we tend to
develop at our own pace and in our own direction. If
the directions are compatible, if they dovetail or run
in tandem, fine. If, however, they fragment an affair
and cause friction and resentment, it may be time to
go your separate ways.

Should you feel you are hidebound by just such
a relationship and that all your interests and enthusi-
asms are a bone of contention, have the courage to
speak up. You owe it to yourself and your partner to
bring these issues out in the open. That way you may
be able to reach a compromise. You may not. It may
simply be time to move on.

In a similar way a wise parent will know when
it's time for their offspring to take on the challenges
of a wider world. A foolish parent will try to put off
their departure. Don't hinder them. Encourage them
to follow their dreams. Be a rock to which they can
return at any time.

It is important to avoid the danger of living vicar-
iously through your children. This is not to say that
we cannot delight in the new vision of the world that
a child's view can create for us. But even while the
children are still at home we need to keep up our
own interests, retain a sense of identity and not just

degenerate into being someone's parent. Otherwise, when they go, the gap left by the parting can seem almost impossible to bear. In hanging on, you make their leaving a painful procedure rather than a natural rite of passage.

Prepare your children, and yourself, for this departure throughout their growing years. Loosen the strings gradually, and when the time comes, wave them goodbye fondly in the calm assurance that they will visit often, eventually bringing their own children with them.

Cling, whine, play on their guilt feelings and, when they do go, you may never see them again.

As we age, our needs change. When we are young, we need *everything*. The latest video, the best trainers, the most up-to-date, trendiest, fashion-conscious threads. We desperately want to make an impression, to be special. The only way we know how to do it is through the things we own. Being acquisitive is part of the process of growing up.

If, however, when we reach maturity, we are still forever acquiring more things – a new car, a bigger house, a younger wife – we may need to reconsider our outlook.

We are not what we own, what we earn, what we do. We are more than the sum of all those things. As we mature, our need to hoard and collect should diminish rather than increase. It is in our ability to be happy with less that true wisdom resides.

This is not to say that there is anything wrong with wealth or that everyone who has it is shallow. The richest people in the world may be the richest in spirit. Only if, supposing they lost their fortunes tomorrow, they could pick themselves up and start over.

You don't need money to be happy. Own your wealth. Don't let it own you.

People who are owned by their wealth are always afraid of losing it. It brings them fear and worry rather than joy. Belongings are chains if you can't do without them.

In my youth, when an older person used to assure me that age had its compensations, I would snort and invite them to 'Name one!' I couldn't think of a single thing that age had to recommend it. Wrinkles and middle-age spread and receding hairlines? Give me a break!

Now that I am older I know that I was looking for my compensations in the wrong place. So let me name not one but several good things which I've discovered about becoming more mature. If you're twenty you may not be too impressed – but try to suspend your judgement. You're not going to be twenty for ever.

The chief pleasure is that I know who I am. And I'm happy with that. I no longer have to make excuses for myself or pretend to be someone I'm not or camouflage myself in the latest creation to get attention. If someone arrives at a party in the same dress as me, I am amused. It doesn't faze me. At twenty I would probably have gone home or hidden in the loo for the rest of the evening.

I've also got to the point where I'm not particularly bothered if someone doesn't like me. You can't please everybody. *I* like me, that's the important thing. I know I am fine, not perfect (thank God) but OK just as I am. What's more, I know that every day (in every way) I'm making progress. There is always more to learn – for all of us.

Lest you get the wrong impression, let me also emphasize that I am not Pollyanna. Neither am I a parsimonious, sanctimonious, smug, self-opinionated, holier-than-thou old fuddy-duddy (except on bad days). I still love good food, sunshine, a glass of red wine, working out, jazz, fine paintings, silk pyjamas, cashmere sweaters, fast cars, foreign travel and men (not necessarily in that order). But I don't *need* them. They are an adjunct to my happiness, not the reason for it. I am who I am. It's enough. Everything else is a bonus.

I can honestly say I wouldn't swap the sweet anticipation with which I now greet each new day for all the desperate, glamorous insecurity of youth.

Just as well, eh? Since there's not much likelihood that I'm going to get the chance!

They say that youth is wasted on the young. I don't believe it. As long as you make the most of it, nothing is ever wasted. Enjoy every second. Embrace every golden opportunity. Only when you *don't* make the most of it does lost youth become a source of regret.

Many of our beliefs were implanted before we were old enough to know any better. They may not even be *our* beliefs at all. They may be misconceptions passed down from parent to child over generations. Or they may be things we simply assimilated from people whom we then respected (our infant teacher), or admired (our first boyfriend – the spotty one who jilted us), or feared (the school bully). From them we may have uploaded the erroneous information that it's bad manners to whistle, or people can't be trusted, or we are natural victims . . . all of which is, of course, rot.

Often we hold on to old beliefs which not only don't serve us, they positively do us harm. Things like . . .

- I'm not good enough.

- I can't do maths.

- That's a man's job.

- I'm too fat, too plain, too stupid.

If beliefs of this sort are stunting your growth or stopping your upward mobility, it's time you reviewed them in the cold light of day and asked yourself honestly, where did they come from? Are they beliefs? Or are they other people's assumptions?

Know this too: beliefs can be changed.

The first step in the process is to question them. So, consider the following.

What are you not good enough for?

Can you add up totals in the supermarket, balance your books, cope with your budget? (What else do we need maths for in real life?)

Are you capable of changing a tyre, a fuse, a light bulb? Have you ever tried?

Are you healthy? Are you alert? Have you as much right to your opinion as any pontificating pillock on TV?

Well then, don't let outmoded beliefs hamstring you. Dissect them. Laugh at them. Throw them out and replace them with versions that encourage rather than hold you back.

See yourself for what you truly are – competent, clever, capable, attractive, *unique*.

Believe it!

Many of the destructive habits we indulge in are a direct result of the insecurity which arises from the unfounded beliefs we hold about ourselves. Deal with the outmoded beliefs and it becomes easier to dispense with the bad habits.

Habits are comfort mechanisms, coping strategies invented by our psyche to alleviate the doubt and fear and unworthiness that gnaw at our guts. At their worst, habits can become addictions.

Things like overeating (or other eating disorders such as anorexia or bulimia), alcoholism, sexual addiction, gambling or watching too much TV are all behaviours that give relief at the time. That they do damage in the long term is not the issue. Habits are the smokescreens which stop you addressing the root problem: your fear of what you perceive to be reality.

Change the reality by changing the beliefs and you can change the habits. Trying to change the habits without attacking the cause will get you nowhere.

Realign your beliefs to encompass the reality of a brave new you. You are not a bad person. You may have some bad habits. But you are not your habits. You *can* let them go. After all, you don't still suck your thumb, do you?

Underpinning all this letting go is compassion again. Not just for ourselves and our past mistakes but also for those whose paths have crossed ours along the way. Allowing beloved people or treasured things to pass out of our life will always be a challenge. Learning to let go with good grace makes space for something equally precious to fill the vacuum.

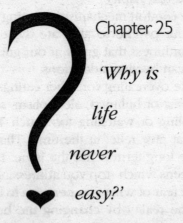

Chapter 25

'Why is life never easy?'

Surviving the downside

There will always be bad times. We cannot control the world. But bad times can be overcome. Our survival depends on our response to the event. If we break under the strain we will go under. If we view the disaster as an opportunity to learn valuable lessons then we will emerge stronger and wiser and better able to face the future.

This is where love comes in. If you love yourself enough and have enough love in your life, you can live through any heartbreak, rise above any defeat. And if you can learn to love those bad times, or at least accept them in the knowledge that they are there for a purpose, then you have come a long way in appreciating that love is present in every experience.

Learning the lessons of betrayal, desertion, divorce

People who betray others can never trust themselves. They deserve our compassion more than our condemnation. They live in a world that few of us would care to inhabit, a dog-eat-dog world where nothing is safe or secure. Think of this if you have been badly betrayed. It may give you a crumb of comfort.

It is difficult, some might say impossible, to forgive – or even understand – someone who has deserted you, trampled on your dreams, broken your heart. Yet it is in our forgiveness and understanding that our salvation lies. Dreams can be rebuilt, broken hearts mended. Your recovery rests in your own hands.

If you have just come out of a difficult relationship the last thing you may want to do is sit down and view the situation objectively. But if you want to sweep aside the debris and leave the way clear for a new start you owe it to yourself to try.

When you have had something done to you, it's so easy to accept yourself as a victim. You need to shake off this image as soon as possible. Because perennial victims are perennially put upon. So unless you want to have the same thing happen again – and again – and again – you would be well advised to learn the lessons that are being forcibly and painfully thrust upon you at this moment. Don't stick your head in the sand and hope they go away. They won't.

Probably the hardest lesson to accept is responsibility for *your* part in the situation.

'But it was all *their* fault,' I hear you wail. 'They left me (or stole my money or beat me up).'

Of course they did. And nobody deserves any of that. But ask yourself, was there anything, even the smallest, teensiest thing you did that could have contributed to it? Love yourself enough to be scrupulously honest. For in your answer lies the pattern of future events.

We are not talking fault here, or blame. We are talking clarity of vision. We are trying to make sure that it's harder for something like this to happen again.

It's easy to be wise after the event and that's what this sort of soul-searching is all about. Yet no matter whether it's easy or not, some people seem to feel it's folly to be wise. They don't choose to look at their own behaviour. They simply want to lay the blame elsewhere and behave in an identical fashion next time round. Then they moan when the same results occur. Is this bad luck – or bad judgement?

If you are in business and you go bankrupt because of bad management and you start another business and you make the same mistakes, you will go bankrupt again. It's as simple as that.

So it is with love. If you always do what you always did, you'll always get what you always got.

The process of gaining wisdom can be a painful one. The sooner you learn the lessons, the sooner the pain will stop. If you don't do your homework you will never graduate. Worse, you'll have to sit through the same unpleasant lessons over and over and over again.

So ask yourself some questions.

Did you see it coming?

Did you contribute to it by ignoring the warning signs?

Do you always choose the same sort of character with whom to be involved?

What was your payback – a lifestyle that was too good to lose, a quiet life, security, freedom from responsibility? What?

We *know* it was all their fault. But ask the questions anyway. Answer them honestly. Forewarned is forearmed.

Now ask yourself another question. Ask yourself what you've gained from the experience? If all you can think of is misery, despair, unhappiness, dig a little deeper. Might you not have gained something in survival techniques, in freedom, in personal choice? And if you haven't could you reframe your thinking to admit those possibilities?

Don't punish yourself. This is all about compassion. The compassion to view yourself honestly and use the information obtained for your recovery. Self-analysis of this sort can only serve you, giving you the courage and awareness to make better choices in the future.

Defeat

You are never defeated until you say you are. While you continue to strive for success, even though it may seem nothing but a constant battle against adversity, you are a hero still. It is when you give up that the battle is lost. Admit defeat and it becomes a reality.

One of the saddest facts in the world is that most people give up just before the breakthrough that would change their lives for the better. Just one more push and they could have had it all.

The difference between success and mediocrity is that successful people *never* give up. They keep on trying. Thomas Edison is reputed to have failed ten thousand times before he eventually invented the light bulb. Most of us would have given up after the fourth or fifth attempt. When asked how he'd felt about all those failures, he said he hadn't failed, he'd just found ten thousand ways *not* to invent a light bulb.

Love allows you to believe in yourself to the point where you will never give up. Love yourself enough to keep on trying.

Age is no barrier to success. In today's youth culture it's easy to believe that if you haven't made it by thirty you've missed the boat. Not so. Colonel Sanders invented the famous chicken recipe that made him a fortune when he was seventy-six. Mary Wesley was over sixty before she wrote her first best-selling novel (and is still writing best-selling novels twenty years on). Whatever your age or experience, persistence pays off. Just because you haven't hit the jackpot yet doesn't mean you never will.

You may not be ready for it. Early success can be a dangerous commodity. Think of all the young people who have hit the top before they were wise enough to deal with the reality that money doesn't always buy happiness and that more is not necessarily better, and who have paid the ultimate price. The truth is, if you reach the top too soon, there may be nowhere to go but down. Climbing to the highest rung on the ladder of life may be a struggle. Staying there is altogether harder.

Your dream may be as simple as a house in the

country or as complicated as inventing an answer to the greenhouse effect. Whatever . . . don't give up. It's in the aspiration that we prove our genius.

Dealing with rejection

The important thing to remember about rejection is that it's always about the other person's limitations, never about one's own.

A person who rejects love, freely given, is lacking in the ability to accept – and consequently to give love back. That is their problem – not yours. They are afraid of intimacy, unwilling to commit. They are isolated and insulated. Ultimately they are rejecting themselves and their capacity to love.

And there is no need for you to accept any rejection as proof that there is something wrong with you. There isn't. Because one person doesn't love you, agree with your views, accept you as an equal or choose you for a job, doesn't mean you are any less lovable, your opinions any less valid, or that you are unequal or incapable. They have their own agenda. You can't please all of the people all of the time.

It's your reaction to the rejection that does the harm. Don't judge yourself. Other people's opinions are only opinions, they are not the law. Don't allow a single rejection to colour your entire life, persuade you to give up on a dream or make you turn your back on love.

They say that when the gods wish to punish us, they answer our prayers. In this instance, might not the gods have been looking after your interests? You may well have outgrown the lover, hated the coveted job. Look honestly at the situation. Dare to be open to the possibility that something better will come along.

Feelings of rejection often begin in childhood. If this feeling of parental rejection has haunted you all your adult life, now is the time to lay the ghost once and for all. Now that you are a grown-up, allow yourself to see your parents for what they are. Human beings like yourself, doing the best they can. Often just acknowledging this makes it much easier to reframe one's attitudes to other perceived rejections and put them in perspective.

A rejection is only a rejection when you receive it as such. Try to see the hurt behind the other person's actions. Realize that you are neither lacking nor to blame. Rejecting yourself by believing that you are not worthy of love is the ultimate rejection. Learn the lessons of this book and you will know that as long as you love yourself and have compassion for the other party, no one can ever reject you again.

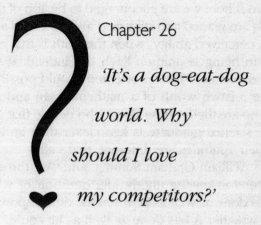

Chapter 26

'It's a dog-eat-dog world. Why should I love my competitors?'

Competition is consistently billed as something which brings out the best in people. It is a modern-day myth that is as harmful to a civilized society as it is blatantly untrue.

Competition on the football pitch leads to conflict on the terraces. Competition between rival gangs leads to disorder on the streets. Competition between religious sects leads to terrorism and sectarian violence. Taken to its logical conclusion, competition leads to the conflagration of war and the obscenity of genocide.

So, does competition bring out the best in us or is it more likely to encourage the basest elements in human nature?

Being the best

The erroneous supposition that to be the best we must be better than others starts early. As soon as we get into school we are encouraged to be 'top of the class'. We are graded and streamed and classified according to perceived ability, when the truth is that every human being is unique. Each has individual strengths and talents. What set of criteria could possibly grade the relative worth of a mathematician and an artist? Who are the faceless 'they' who decide that a domestic science graduate is less clever than an engineer? Their aptitudes are different, that's all.

William Graham Sumner said, 'We throw all our attention on the utterly idle question of whether A has done as well as B, when the only important thing is whether A has done as well as he could.'

The tragedy of a system based on competition is that so few people win. All the rest are labelled as losers. Instead of being encouraged to 'be the best they can be', they are stamped 'not as good as'. The stigma can last for life.

Not everyone has the self-belief of a Winston Churchill who, branded a duffer at school, went on to become one of the greatest inspirational leaders of the century. And thank heavens Albert Einstein took scant notice of his less than complimentary term reports and went on thinking for himself.

Competition is divisive in the extreme. The so-called bright sparks assume feelings of lofty superiority that may close them off from the practicalities of life. It's a well-documented fact that a considerable number of MENSA members are so un-streetwise that they are incapable of making a living. Their IQs may be astronomical but in life terms they are less able than any hired hand. Being brainy and being smart are not necessarily the same.

Meanwhile the less academically able are marked in their own minds as useless. Lack of self-worth can lead to delinquency and hopelessness. Sayings like 'You might as well be last as be second' encourage people who know they are not going to be first not to bother to be anything at all. They have been taught that what they have to offer is of no value.

Learning should be a joyful experience. The gaining of knowledge, the development of character, the unfolding of the mind are all part of the attainment of wisdom. Yet success in the examination system may depend solely on the conning of information by rote, whether it is understood or not. Worse, pupils are unlikely to ask questions about a theory they have not grasped if they fear looking foolish before their peers or being told that they are stupid by a teacher.

The basic trial-and-error system which is fundamental to the discovery of new processes seems to have scant space in the modern classroom. This is a scandalous waste of brainpower. For children flourish in an atmosphere of unthreatening encouragement. And a love of knowledge learned in an enabling atmosphere lasts for life.

Raising the standards

The only person we need to compete with is ourself. The constant raising of our own standards encourages us to do better than we did before, not better than someone else has done.

The most effective educators recognize this and

strive to bring out the best in *all* their students by encouraging each individual to work at a level commensurate with their current ability. They are lavish in their praise and minimal and constructive in their criticism. They motivate and inspire. They draw out the latent genius in all of us by establishing a belief in possibilities.

A good teacher never uses fear as an incentive or competition as a spur, knowing both to be counterproductive. Fear makes the mind close down. And naked competition encourages that fear – fear of rejection, fear of reprisals, fear of scorn, fear of punishment, fear of not being good enough.

Where is the love in this equation? Because it is love, and belief in the human spirit, that has provided some of the most spectacular results of recent years in urban ghetto areas in the United States, where inspired teachers have succeeded in fashioning A students from youngsters previously graded as illiterate delinquents. Even the most recalcitrant child responds better to the carrot than the stick. The thirst for knowledge is endemic in all of us – provided it isn't driven out by discouragement and disapproval.

Love is the greatest teacher of all. Knowledge and fulfilment are the inherent right of everyone, not just the privileged few. That same surge of adrenaline which comes from winning can just as easily be triggered by the sudden understanding of a mathematical equation or grasping of a scientific theory. It doesn't *have* to come from beating someone else to the post. It shouldn't. Beating is the last refuge of the bully and taking your success at someone else's expense is the opposite of civilized behaviour.

There is plenty of success for everyone – including you. But if you have clawed your way to the top over the bodies of vanquished rivals you will wear an uneasy crown. Your belief in competition will have left you constantly looking over your shoulder, fearful of who is coming up behind.

If you want to inspire loyalty, and sleep easy in your bed, the secret is to encourage rather than dampen the next generation's aspirations. Share your experience with them. Be generous with your help. Fuel their enthusiasm, then stand back and watch the result. They are not a threat, they are the future. They want your experience, not your job.

The worst and least efficient managers are the ones who refuse to delegate for fear of being replaced. They are also the ones who *are* replaced – or who burn out – soonest. And no one is sorry to see them go.

Share the wealth

The greatest reward for an educator is to have taught the pupil so well that he eventually outshines his master and takes the work to another level.

This is the theory behind the mentor system. Well established in the USA, it is rapidly gaining credence in Britain. Older, more experienced experts in their field take a younger acolyte under their wing and show them the ropes. This precludes the newcomer from having to reinvent the wheel and start, as their mentors did, from scratch. By eliminating the trial-and-error process the new generation's education is speeded up. The pupil also absorbs, not only the theoretical and practical aspects of the skill, but also the enthusiasm of their instructor and a feeling of connection with him or her. The pupil's success is the teacher's triumph rather than a cause for paranoia or concern. This one-to-one, master/pupil relationship is not a new idea. The principle goes back centuries. It's good to see it make a comeback.

Networking

It is in everybody's interest to get as much knowledge out into the world as possible. Knowledge opens up the dark corners, shines a light on ignorance and bigotry. It is the messenger of love and, as such, it shouldn't be rationed. If you have specialized knowledge, don't hoard it or be stingy with your expertise. Pass it on. Hand it round. Your reputation is only enhanced by generosity.

The lesson of the Druids

Once knowledge was the prerogative of the few, the priests and wise men and shamans of the tribe. They used it to manipulate and influence the uneducated and superstitious many. Information was guarded jealously and distributed sparingly – usually by word of mouth to novices who were sworn to secrecy.

The 'mysteries', as they were known, included an intimate knowledge of star systems which allowed the wise men to predict eclipses and develop a calendar from which they could chart the seasons and perfect a system for planting crops. To the uninitiated this appeared to be magic. They believed that their priests commanded the very heavens as well as governing the earth.

The Druidic traditions were painstakingly committed to memory over long years of study by the chosen few. Punishment for betraying their vows of silence was draconian. Flayed and walled up alive, the miscreant endured an excruciating death. But because none of their wisdom was ever written down it was not preserved for the benefit of future generations. With the coming of the 'White Christ', the body of knowledge evaporated within half a century, lost to the world through the erroneous belief in competition.

Co-operation

This is the age of *instant* communication. Anyone who owns a word processor has access to virtually anything, from the contents of the world's libraries to the most up-to-date scientific data. Competition through specialized knowledge has become a thing of the past. We must share what we know or be shunted to the sidelines.

Co-operation rather than competition has become the order of the day. More and more people are realizing that if they co-operate with others, then what they have to offer, be it services or products or knowledge or the hand of friendship, can only reach a wider audience. Together we can make giant steps forward.

Co-operation is competition's caring twin. More humane than its sibling, it is also much more effective. Co-operation means never being tricky or trying to get the upper hand; working for the good of both parties in negotiation rather than trying to gain unfair advantage; taking on the responsibility of training the next generation; acknowledging the compliment if that generation takes the work a stage higher than you could have done. Co-operation has won as many medals as competition ever did.

Sport

Sport is founded on competition. Nowhere is it more entrenched. We are taught that the competitive spirit is what breaks records and wins matches. Yet recent research has shown that competition *doesn't* improve performance. Quite the contrary.

Competition nerves frequently impair performance levels. Someone has to lose. Losing is seen as failure. Fear of failure can make an athlete perform way below their best and produce the very thing they dread most.

The most successful athletes are those who concentrate on their own performance and who are able to evaluate how well they've done against their own criteria, whether they've won the competition or not. Their aspiration is to produce a personal best rather than humiliate their adversaries through defeat.

A generous winner will always have friends and admirers. A person who wins at any cost will have few people to commiserate with him when he loses.

By all means compete with yourself to raise standards. Constantly try to improve the products or services you offer. Aim for excellence in all that you do. But treat your opponents with respect.

Ten ways to connect rather than compete

- Share the wealth – your knowledge, money, expertise – for the benefit of all concerned.

- Try to create win/win situations in any negotiation, whether at work, at home or among friends. Offer choices rather than dictate terms.

- Remember that networking is not about grabbing the advantage, it's about give and take. Be generous and others will be happy to reciprocate. If you are greedy, they'll soon catch on and cut you out.

- If you can't avoid a competitive situation at least honour and respect your adversary. This is the spirit on which the original Olympic Games were based.

- Be the best you can be, don't strive to be better than anyone else.

- Always encourage a desire for knowledge in anyone who asks for it.

- Be generous in success. Don't gloat.

- Be gracious in defeat. Don't say you were robbed.

- Be open-handed in your congratulations when others succeed.

- Be glad of others' success, knowing that any achievement can only be of benefit to us all.

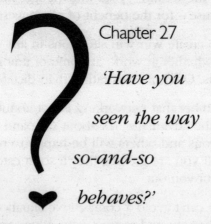

Chapter 27

'Have you seen the way so-and-so behaves?'

Judgementalism is such an insidious thing that it's almost impossible to discuss it without becoming, well, judgemental. The worst thing about judgementalism, a holier-than-thou attitude that is at once unpleasant and deeply harmful, is that most of us indulge in it as though it were our God-given right.

What someone wears, how they behave, their morals, views or lifestyle are frankly none of our business, provided none of these things impinges on our reality and does us actual harm.

But we love to make it our business all the same.

Sitting in judgement on a friend, enemy, celebrity or society figure gives us a perverted sense of power. As though our opinion was impartial and important, when in fact it is neither.

The thrill of passing on the malicious tit-bit has reached epic proportions in the modern media. There is a kind of unholy power attached to gossip columns in that the spoken word, solidified in print, takes on the cloak of truth even though it may be the very opposite. Hedda Hopper, acid columnist and failed actress, was once the most powerful woman in Hollywood quite simply because a malicious mention in her weekly copy could make or break even a big star's career.

And no amount of apologies, usually buried in very small print towards the back of the paper (even though the original scurrilous story carried banner headlines on the front page), can undo the damage. We believe what we want to believe. And it seems we want to believe the worst.

Nowadays almost anything, no matter how unsavoury, can be reported under the hypocritical clarion of the public's 'need to know', when the only real consideration is how many newspapers the latest scandal will sell.

This is me being judgemental about the media. Let me try to redress the balance by saying there are many excellent investigative newshounds around who expose crime and corruption in high places (and low) and whose work uncovers issues which need to be addressed. But lately it seems that there is no secret too dire, no corner too dank, no personal moment too private for some unprincipled hack to stick his nose or his microphone into it. This is journalism as judgementalism. It panders to the lowest common denominator in human nature and reduces us to the level of voyeurs.

Whatever happened to the good news? Because

there is good news out there. More good than bad. Most adults are hard-working and law-abiding. Most teenagers would rather help an old lady across the road than pinch her purse. Most children are in school and not playing hookey. More people die on the roads than from drug abuse. But apparently the devil not only has the best tunes, he also gets the most publicity.

This is not to deny that outrages do occur and if viewing horror spurs us to do something about it (as with Bob Geldof and Band Aid), then fair enough. If it only makes us feel helpless in the face of misery or dulls our sensitivities to violence then what possible good can it do?

And if it gives some unprincipled terrorist a load of free publicity for his benighted cause, are we not playing into his hands or, worse, colluding in his outrages?

We may feel we cannot do much individually to stop media influence. Of course we can. To alter your own perception of reality all you have to do is press that off-button, cancel the daily paper, start to tune in to life rather than cyberspace. You'll be astounded how much better and safer and happier you feel almost immediately. If we did this in our thousands, the media would soon lose its grip on our outlook.

At the very least we can take responsibility for our own attitudes, stop getting pleasure from the misfortunes of others, focus on the up rather than the downbeat for a change.

Envy

When you hear of someone doing well are you delighted for them? Does it give you hope? Success is the living proof of what a human being can achieve. And you are a human being. So it stands to reason that if one person can gain their heart's desire, so can you.

But too many people, when they hear of another's success, are riddled with envy.

'Why couldn't it be *me*?' they say. 'Why should he have it when I can't?' Or they pass on the opinion that the person concerned must have come by their good fortune through nefarious means, rather than by hard work or genuine ability. And if the winner's fortunes take a downturn, oh – the glee! 'Have you heard the latest? So-and-so have split up, they're repossessing the house, the receivers have been called in.'

If you know someone who behaves like this (perhaps even intimately!) ask what they gain by it. If another person had *not* won an Oscar or made a success of their business or married the love of their life, would it have made *you* any better off?

Be glad for other people's good fortune. Put your efforts into building yourself up rather than tearing them down. That way there's more chance that you too will get the chance at happiness.

Spite

Spite is an offshoot of envy. It shows itself in vandalism or the wilful destruction of someone else's property. The kind of behaviour which prompts someone to run a coin across a Rolls-Royce's paintwork, with no more justification than that if they can't own something so beautiful then they will spoil it for anyone who does.

Very few people who own Rolls-Royces get them as birthday presents. Most of them work hard for years, rising through the ranks, grafting all the hours God gave, and have at last come to the point where they can afford to buy themselves something special as a reward. The fact that you may want a Rolls-Royce, too, doesn't automatically mean you deserve one. Defacing such a work of art probably proves that you don't. Meanness of spirit is no qualification for riches.

Malicious gossip

Here's a modern parable which I heard recently.

There was a woman who, envious of a young girl's beauty, blackened her character in the community by saying that she had been away to have an illegitimate child when in reality she had been caring for a sick relative in a neighbouring village.

When the girl came back she was horrified to find herself shunned by her neighbours and abandoned by her fiancé. And, since no one would talk to her, she couldn't find out why.

Eventually, after months of psychological torture, she had cause to do a good turn for the woman who had started all the trouble. Overcome by a fit of conscience, the woman confessed, asked to be forgiven and promised to undo the mischief.

In reply, the girl took her up to the top of the church tower. She brought a feather pillow with her and when they got to the top she slit it open and shook the feathers out into the air. They floated down like snow, carried by the four winds far outside the village enclaves to all parts of the countryside.

The girl handed her tormentor the empty pillow-case.

'When you can refill this with every feather,' she said, 'you can undo the harm you have done.'

Remember those feathers next time you're tempted to blacken a reputation for the sake of an interesting piece of lunchtime gossip. Mud sticks. It's too late to say you're sorry after the event.

Criticism as bile

It's so easy to be a critic. Seeing the faults in something is much simpler than creating an original concept from scratch. So criticism should be, as much as is humanly possible, constructive.

That's not to say you should lie. It isn't constructive to tell your best friend that an outfit looks great on her if it actually makes her look terrible. But too often criticism is used as a way to make ourselves look clever at someone else's expense.

Never offer feedback at all unless it's asked for. It is presumptuous to assume you know better than someone else what they should do, say or wear. However, if someone does ask, by all means be honest. But try to temper your judgement with mercy. If your opinions are less than complimentary, at least soften the blow by emphasizing the good points first.

In the case of the friend and the frock, for instance, better to say, 'I love the colour, it just matches your eyes, but to be honest I don't think the shape does you justice,' rather than coming out with a blunt

'It makes you look like a sack tied in the middle.' If you strengthen a person's sense of self-worth initially, you are much less likely to hurt their feelings.

Creative artists are particularly vulnerable to negative criticism. Producing a work of the imagination is like giving birth. There is sweat and blood and pain involved. Is it any wonder then that the creator may defend their work as they would a child under attack? So if you have a talented friend or offspring, be careful that you encourage rather than deflate. Many a creative spark has been completely extinguished by harsh and ill-judged comment.

Criticism can be a force for improvement or a deadly weapon. Use it sparingly and with grace.

Mental bullying

The unacceptable way to prop up a floundering ego is by making others look small. Just as sarcasm is the lowest form of wit, so self-aggrandisement at another's expense is never justified. People who behave like this are feared but seldom loved.

If you are at the mercy of a psychological bully, understanding that they have a much lower opinion of themselves than they have of you is often enough to help you extricate yourself from their influence. If you can extend this understanding to compassion for their pain, you will have won a great moral victory. There's no need to feel smug. Just walk away.

Physical bullying

On the other hand, if you are being physically abused, realize that such behaviour can never come from a loving intent, only from hate and fear. And that no amount of apologies or declarations of love after the event can make it right. Refuse to accept such behaviour. Run for your life.

People stay in abusive situations either because it's all they've ever known or because they feel they aren't worthy of any other kind of relationship. Recognize that abuse has nothing to do with *your* unworthiness, and everything to do with the abuser's. Everyone deserves to be loved. Love yourself enough to get help. It's out there.

Hypocrisy

Hypocrisy is one of the most unpleasant forms of judgementalism.

You don't have to approve of bad behaviour. But ask yourself, would you like the press camping on your doorstep, going through your private letters, sifting through your past exploits? Are you so squeaky clean that you wouldn't have a momentary twinge about something (maybe many things) if someone suddenly appeared on your doorstep with a big red book and announced that 'This is your life'? Are there absolutely *no* skeletons in your particular cupboard?

Well then. Better perhaps to live and let live? There but for the grace of God go all of us.

Judgementalism kills compassion. It is narrow and mean-minded. It makes us suspicious of even the purest motives. It is represented by a sneer. It is the opposite of connection, the antithesis of love.

It is most damaging when it is used against ourselves. When we constantly judge ourselves as wanting, we lack the resources to give ourselves the very love that would allow us to be everything we can be.

Recovery begins when we can say at last, 'I'm all right just as I am,' and mean it. Compassion for self leads to compassion for others. Recognizing that you are not perfect and perhaps never will be, but that every day you're improving, brings with it the ability to recognize the same striving in everyone.

We are not our brother's keeper. If we concentrated on sorting out our own hang-ups and left our brothers to sort out theirs, there would be a lot less strife in the world.

So next time you feel the urge to pass judgement on some unfortunate celebrity who never did you a button of harm but who has just happened to choose an unsuitable new boyfriend or make a serious error in sartorial taste, ask yourself this: Given similar circumstances, would I have done any better?

Being aware of your judgementalism is half the battle. The other half is defeating it. It takes constant vigilance.

Below are a handful of memory joggers that might help. If you catch yourself slipping into the judgemental mire copy one of them out a hundred times. Repetition is the mother of remembrance. And practice makes perfect (well, nearly).

Homework

- It's their problem and they'll deal with it.

- They're doing the best they can.

- I'm delighted they have been so successful.

- Everybody's entitled to their opinion.

- I forgive myself.

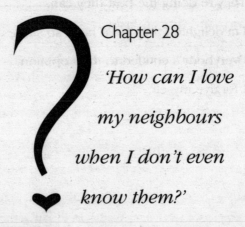

Chapter 28

'How can I love

my neighbours

when I don't even

know them?'

These days it's not only possible, but downright usual, to live in a block of flats for years without having an inkling of who your neighbours are. What else could account for the horror stories of people being found in their homes, having been dead for six months, and no one even missing them?

Years ago, it would never have happened. People were born, brought up and died in the same street, generation after generation. They knew each other's histories and were in and out of each other's houses as a regular routine. Neighbours baby-sat for each other, kept an eye on the cat if someone went on holiday, knew who was marrying whom, wet each baby's head and attended every family wake. People stuck together. Communal support and neighbourliness were taken as a matter of course.

The rot set in in the fifties when high-rise blocks replaced slums and bombsites left over from the Second World War. They were hailed as the architectural wonders of the brave new world. But unfortunately they broke up whole communities. In human terms people found that an inside toilet was no substitute for a helping hand in time of trouble.

These concrete columns alienated rather than involved. People who wouldn't have thought twice about popping two doors down to borrow a cup of sugar found themselves reluctant to go two floors up for the same purpose.

The sense of displacement went further. With no front step to scrub, no windows to clean, folk lost their feeling of individual ownership. They were all lumped together in a soulless structure that wasn't even particularly user-friendly. Not only the elderly but young mums with small children could become trapped in this kind of living accommodation, unable to go out if the lifts broke down, cut off from even a back yard, let alone a garden, in which to play or take the sun.

There are still country communities where everyone knows everyone else, where the postman and milkman and local bobby provide a communal link and a friendly face. But cities can be desperately lonely places. The constant crush of humanity – on the streets, in the supermarkets, the tube, bus or train – only serves to point up personal isolation. Being alone in a crowd is very different from being alone on a windswept moor or an isolated beach – and much more destabilizing. Is it any wonder that graffiti and vandalism are rife? It's not easy to take pride in something from which one feels spiritually disconnected.

In such a situation there is a tendency to huddle in packs, drawn together by a common religion, race, age, sexual orientation or political obsession. Misconceptions spring up between groups. Unwholesome untruths proliferate. All teenagers are vandals. Anyone over fifty should be put down. Blacks steal. Homosexuals are a danger to our children.

Fear and mistrust polarize even further. Some elderly people are terrified to leave the house, certain that the minute they step outside the door they'll be mugged. Young mothers, cut off from the extended family which would once have lightened the maternal load, become depressed and irritable and take it out on their children.

We need to remember that everyone is our neighbour. Not only the person who lives next door. We all inhabit the same small planet, breathe the same air, drink the same water. We all have a responsibility to and for each other. Whether we like it or not, unless we reach out and make contact, we will continue to be lonely and isolated.

The way to break the alienation cycle is to start with a smile, a greeting, an offer of help. Such a gesture can bring surprising and immediate results. People *want* to be neighbourly. Mostly they simply lack the practice, or are afraid of rejection, or don't know how to go about it. They are worried they will be thought nosey or interfering, anxious that they shouldn't be seen as a nuisance. So the smile dies on the lips, the greeting remains unsaid, the offer is never made.

Someone has to take a lead. Why shouldn't it be you?

Neighbourliness doesn't mean constantly interrupting someone who you know works from home.

Nor is it about arriving unannounced and outstaying your welcome. It's about being thoughtful and taking a genuine interest in the other person's welfare. It also means respecting someone's privacy if they want to be left to themselves.

So, how do you start?

Making contact

- Borrow that cup of sugar – even if you don't need one – and return it next day. Somewhere along the line, introduce yourself.

- Use the season of goodwill in the way it was intended. Send a card to everyone on the stairwell/block/avenue. ('All at No. 2' – or whatever.) That way, at least they'll know your name. And when they send one back, you'll know theirs. It's a beginning.

- Invite at least the people on either side (or above and below) for drinks on Christmas morning. Next year, extend it to the two on either side of them. By the end of the decade you'll know almost everybody in the building or on the street.

- If you have a car and are going to the super-market, ask an elderly neighbour if they'd like a lift. Not everyone has a car. No need to dog each other's tracks. You can split up and meet at the checkout. What's a chore for you may be an outing for them.

- If you're in trouble (locked out, can't reach the

fuse box, you've cut yourself and have run out of Elastoplast) – ask for help. Most people are only too glad to oblige.

- If there's a young couple in the block who never get out, offer to babysit now and again.

- If you're living alone and there's another single person nearby, ask whether they'd like to go to a movie or for a walk in the park on a sunny day.

Don't wait for others to come to you. Have the courage and the compassion to make the first move. Invariably you'll find that, once the initial suspicions have been laid to rest, most people will be only too happy to reciprocate.

When they do, make sure you maintain good relations by being a good neighbour.

Neighbourly no-nos

- Don't play your music so loud it shakes the rafters. Not everyone shares your taste. Be especially sensitive to neighbours' eardrums in the summer when all the windows are open.

- Don't allow your dog to foul the footpath or communal gardens where children play.

- Don't allow your children to trample on flower beds or vandalize stairwells.

- If you're having a party, warn the neighbours with a note through the letterbox (and an invitation if you know them). Set a time limit and make sure it's on a night when everyone can sleep in in the morning. If the neighbours have children and you know the bash is going to be loud and long, hire a hall!

- Don't hoover or move heavy furniture or hammer late at night or early in the morning.

- If you have parquet flooring, take your shoes off when you come in. Stilettos can sound like a herd of elephants to the unfortunate occupant downstairs.

- Don't rev up your car to announce your departure or arrival.

- Don't buy your teenager a drum kit for his/her birthday.

In the wider analysis, loving your neighbour means trusting and allowing others to be trustworthy. It means addressing your prejudices and treating everyone as an equal.

Trusting is not about taking your life in your hands by walking down a dark, unlit alley on your own late at night or tempting providence by parking your brand new car in a ghetto or allowing a stranger into your home without checking ID. Good sense should also prevail.

What trusting *is* about is understanding that the territory may be the same but that everyone's map of it is different and that just because someone has an alternative religious belief or sexual inclination, it doesn't make them a bad person.

Ignorance, fear of the unknown and religious bigotry have caused more conflict and carnage than anything else in history. You don't need to agree with your neighbour to respect their viewpoint. Everyone has a right to their beliefs, no matter how different they may be from our own.

All major religions are based on universal love and understanding. Fundamentalism disallows understanding of other's beliefs no matter which religion it purports to represent. In the end all rules are man-made. Closed minds are always divisive. Respect and honour your neighbour's beliefs and views. Beneath colour, race and creed we are all human beings and all our blood runs red.

Loving your neighbour doesn't mean patronizing him or her. Any communication should come through genuine compassion and a desire to find common ground.

Showing respect

- Honour experience. Never speak to an elderly person as though they were losing their marbles.

- Respect youth. Don't address a child, no matter how young, in baby talk. At best it means they have to learn the language twice. Once for choo-choo, once for train. A child's mind is like a sponge. Allow it to soak up English (or Spanish or Chinese), not rubbish.

- Avoid closet homophobia. Homosexuals are just people. Like heterosexuals they can be nice or nasty, good friends or bad enemies. Treat them as you would anyone else – with tolerance and affection.

- Ditto anyone whose skin is a different shade. A person is a person and ultimately we all sprang from a common mother.

- Never speak to a physically challenged individual as though they were educationally sub-normal. Physical and mental disability are two different things.

- For that matter, never speak to a mentally challenged person in a patronizing way. Tone of voice is more important than content. A loving tone will reach any level of understanding.

- Don't argue about religion. This is an area in which we are each entitled to our own point of view.

- Don't assume that every homeless person is a useless layabout who ought to 'get a decent job'.

- Or that anyone who hasn't got a decent job is an inveterate scrounger living off the tax you pay. Be glad that you can afford to pay the tax. Would you live at the bottom of the social heap out of choice?

- Don't assume that everyone who went to public school is a chinless wonder who gets drunk on champagne and expects Daddy to bail him out when he smashes up a restaurant.

- Or that everyone who went to a secondary modern is a vandalizing oik who spends his leisure time sniffing glue and going to raves (when he's not beating up little old ladies of course).

- Don't assume that anyone with money is a crook, a hardcase who has got it by exploiting others or a lucky bastard who won the lottery.

- Rest assured that 'foreigners' are not here to steal the bread out of our mouths or take over the country. They are not dirty or ignorant. They do not sleep twenty to a room (unless forced to by some venal, indigenous landlord). They are here to make a life for themselves in the country that we were lucky enough to be born in. Most have a strong family structure, work hard and speak more than one language (how many do you speak?). Their culture can only enrich ours by its diversity.

- Finally, never, ever, under any circumstances, call *anyone* 'dear'. It is the most condescending word in the language.

If you look back over the three lists in this chapter you will find that none of the items mentioned calls for financial investment. So, the good news is that good neighbourliness is free! You don't have to be privileged to practise it. What you do need is a reappraisal of attitude and some simple loving kindness.

Being a good neighbour simply means treating others as you would want them to treat you. Respecting their privacy. Honouring their beliefs. It means never being opportunistic or rude to anyone who's not in a position to answer back. It means not taking advantage of another's good nature. In short, neighbourliness is represented by kindness, consid-eration and good old-fashioned courtesy. Being open-minded, open-handed, open-hearted.

It's a simple formula. Hard to live up to? Perhaps, but not impossible.

A positive template for a better future.

Chapter 29

'Surely nobody loves their ❤ enemy?'

'Always forgive your enemies, nothing annoys them so much,' said Oscar Wilde. The concept of turning the other cheek requires no more complex coping strategies than those we have already discussed in other chapters – in theory. Taking the initiative, making the first move, proffering the olive branch, understanding the other person's point of view, allowing love to heal the wound are all approaches that apply here. It's just that it's much more difficult to live up to them in the face of spite, unfairness or downright injustice. The natural reaction is to leap to our own defence, to hit back, to *hurt* back. This is what an animal would do. But hopefully we have evolved beyond the animal stage. As thinking organisms we should be able to work out a more productive way to behave. Otherwise where will it all end?

Violence unchecked escalates into revenge, vendetta, war, chaos. If we shoot first and ask questions afterwards we will never break the cycle. Our future will be as bloody as our past.

The answer lies in our individual efforts to love our enemies, no matter what. There is an old saying that a 'kind word turneth away wrath'. And it is really very difficult to sustain a furious confrontation when faced with someone who simply refuses to be drawn into an argument. This is the point at which to stop all those wars happening: at the very beginning. Once a situation has reached the stage where backing down means losing face the disagreement has gained its own momentum. There's nowhere to go but down.

Compassion for those who use us badly is the way out of the gutter and up to the stars – for all of us. The simplest way to stimulate that compassion is to realize how unhappy really nasty people are. This helps us to feel sorry for them, rather than furious at their behaviour.

Mean people are miserable. Why? Because positive energy gives life and negative energy drains.

You've proved this yourself. Think of the last time you did a good deed – not to gain recognition, but simply for the joy of doing it. The secret lies in that word, joy. Didn't you feel exhilarated? Wasn't it a charge? Now think about the last time you did a bad deed, lost your temper, deliberately upset someone's plans or spoke to someone sharply, not because they deserved it but just because you were in a foul mood. How did you feel then? My guess would be that you felt exhausted and depleted after the event. Fury, anger, maliciousness, evil, all take a tremendous toll on our physical and mental states. Rage or actual violence floods the body with a hormone the residue of which, whirling round the bloodstream and settling as acid in the stomach, leaves us with an ache in the solar plexus and a feeling of self-disgust and guilt.

Indulged in too often, unbridled anger (which mostly stems from fear) leads to actual physical changes in the body which can manifest in such life-threatening abnormalities as ulcers, high blood pressure and heart attack. Expressions like 'it made my blood boil' may not be too far from the truth. Think of the typical appearance of someone caught in the throws of a temper tantrum. Face bright red, veins standing out on the forehead, corded neck, clenched fists. Do they look as though they're having a good time?

You have to 'work yourself up' into a fine old fury. It's not a natural or relaxed state. In fact it's as far from homeostasis as you can get. It breaks the body down bit by bit until eventually something snaps.

People riddled by spite and malice, who are constantly trying to gain the upper hand by devious means, who are untrustworthy and untrusting, who cheat and lie and gossip and slander and libel and bully, generally live a much shorter life – and a much more unpleasant one – than a person who is kind and considerate and gentle and trusting.

This is what they mean when they say virtue is its own reward. It's a reward that is beyond price and one that is in your own hands. If only you can learn to be compassionate and love your enemies you will live a longer and happier life.

Defusing an angry situation

- Don't rise to the bait or allow confrontation to escalate. Two people screaming at each other or resorting to fisticuffs never solved anything. If things are getting out of hand, remove yourself from the scene. This is not cowardice – it's good sense. Discretion is the better part of valour. You can confront the problem from a much more sensible perspective when everyone – including you – has calmed down.

- Turn the other cheek but don't turn yourself into a victim. In the face of unfair criticism, speak up. Say, 'I don't accept that about myself.' And *don't*. Stating your truth clearly and without anger often halts the invective in mid flow. Most of all, don't let the criticizer undermine your belief in the rightness of your cause. If you do, you will start to get defensive and the situation will take off in precisely the way that you don't want it to.

- Smile – it's very disarming. It may defuse the situation enough for you to say, 'Now why don't we discuss this like sensible people?'

- Expect the best. People who have painted themselves into an indefensible corner are generally delighted to be allowed to reclaim their lost credibility. Nobody *wants* to be a villain. They just don't know any better. Also it may just be a genuine misunderstanding. Tell them your side of the story. And listen to theirs!

- Try to think of them not as enemies but as wounded souls. Everybody wants to be loved. How much love do you think nasty people experience in their lives? Try to see the hurt behind the action. The cruellest behaviour can often be a cry for help. Don't judge until you know all the facts.

- Act – don't react. Realize it's about *them*, not about you. If someone snaps at you, the natural reaction is to snap back. It's a defence mechanism. It's also a reflex action. Take a deep breath and count to ten before you reply.

- Make sure that you are not getting on your high horse for nothing. If you *have* behaved badly then eventually cosmic justice will catch up with you. In this case there's no excuse. Your 'enemies' may be the good guys after all. If you are in the wrong, apologize and try to make amends.

- Put yourself in their place. If someone is behaving really badly, ask yourself: would you want to live in their universe? What drives them to such extremes? Insecurity? Lack of self-worth? Remembrance of past abuse? Inability to trust or commit? Wherever it is that the anger, spite or bile is coming from, it is undoubtedly going to make them feel much worse on a day-to-day basis than they are making you feel at this moment. You can forgive and forget (yes, you *can*). They have to live with it.

- Speak your piece firmly. Don't lose your rag or

you've lost the battle. If you go out to a restaurant and the service and the soufflé are lousy and the management couldn't care less, insist on your rights in a clear, concise manner. Try not to splutter, turn purple or throw the offending item at the waiter. Remember, he didn't cook it – he's only the go-between. He's probably not being as polite as he might be because he always has to take the blame for the chef's lousy cooking. The chef may be having an off-day. His wife may have left him that morning.

- Try not to think of it as a battle but as an honest exchange of views. There are two sides to every situation. Having stated yours – you want another soufflé or some other form of compensation (such as your money back) – allow the other side to state theirs. If you sweep out in high dudgeon, throwing your glass at the manager on the way, you will have done nothing but give yourself indigestion and put yourself in the wrong. And you still won't have had any dinner.

- Repetition reaps rewards. So, repeat over and over, 'I'd like another soufflé please, this one's burned. I'd like another soufflé please, this one's burned. I'd like another soufflé please, this one's burned.' Don't allow yourself to be drawn into an argument about the price of eggs, the difficulty of getting good staff these days or the fact that the real chef has flu and this one's just a temp. All those things are *their* problem. Yours is simply that 'I'd like another soufflé please, this one's burned.'

- Be open to feedback. If you are being criticized or maligned, is there any justification for the accusations? Is there any truth *whatever* in what's being said? If there's even a grain and you take note of that truth and act upon it, something positive will have come out of even the ugliest confrontation. Don't take refuge in injured innocence if you're not actually as innocent as you would like to be. By acting on the feedback you will ensure that there's less chance of such a situation happening in the future.

  However, this doesn't mean allowing a partner or rival to persuade you that you are in the wrong if you're not. Weigh up any feedback honestly. If it *isn't true*, you don't have to accept it.

In the face of corporate indifference, rampant bureaucracy or sheer bloody-mindedness, tell yourself that it's not the situation but *your reaction* to it that makes the difference.

Remind yourself often that nothing has the power to irritate you, unless you give it your consent.

To love your enemy you don't have to forfeit your right to fairness. It's the feeling that you are a cog in a wheel, a worthless speck over which ruthless people can trample at will, which allows desperation to escalate to the point where one does something one regrets, like losing one's temper or lashing out at someone who has no control over the situation (as with the waiter and the soufflé above). Such a reaction reduces you to the level of your adversary.

Know that you are not helpless. You have rights. Pursue them through the proper channels. Insist on justice. Get that soufflé or get a refund – before you leave the restaurant. Loving your enemies doesn't mean allowing anyone to step on your face. If someone abuses you in print (or on air), insist on an apology in print (or on air). Photocopy (or tape) the apology and send a copy to anyone whose bad opinion my affect your future employment or good name.

And don't allow your certainty that you are in the right (if you *are* in the right, that is) to be swayed by the statement that you 'are the first person who has ever complained'. In the first place, this is undoubtedly an exaggeration. In the second place, if the last person who received such bad service, shoddy treatment or was the victim of such malpractice had complained then you wouldn't be having to put up with it and therefore you are doing the next person to enter that particular facility, shop or eating establishment a favour in advance. And third, if you influence the people involved to think about and perhaps improve their standards or behaviour, you are also doing *them* a favour in setting them on the road to excellence.

Which, providing you get your soufflé, is a win/win situation in anybody's book.

Loving your enemy is all about win/win situations. Like all aspects of love it serves both the giver and the receiver. Love has value regardless of where it's directed. In the case of perceived enemies you may not feel that your love is deserved, but it is probably where it is most needed – and ultimately where it will do the most good.

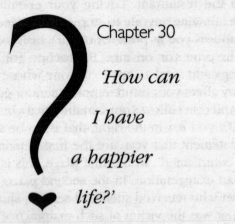

Chapter 30

'How can I have a happier life?'

Some people go through life lamenting that it's a permanent obstacle course. They moan and curse their fate, rail at the unfairness of it all, complain that they weren't born rich or good-looking or lucky. Afraid to take a chance, they sneer at anyone who tries to better themselves, resent anyone who succeeds and dole out their money and love in such minute increments that it never does anyone any good. Including themselves.

And then they wonder why they're miserable.

Life *is* an obstacle course, of course. But what's so bad about that? Leaping fences keeps us on our toes and stops us from dying of boredom. No sooner have we surmounted one molehill than a veritable mountain hoves into view. It seems there's hardly any time to rest on our laurels or take a breather before some new challenge rears up to confront us. You can look at this as exciting or you can look at it as exhausting. It doesn't matter which. The obstacle course is still there.

It's meant to be there. It's in our falling and getting up to try again (or staying in the mud and moaning) that we prove who we are, both to ourselves and to others.

We can either love life or we can loathe it. If we love it, we'll feel fulfilled, despite any trials and tribulations. If we loathe it, even our greatest victories will be clouded by the fear of what comes next.

To make the most of life you need to get your feet wet. Embrace it *all*. Love it all. Let's face it, only a masochist would have a horrible time when he could be enjoying himself.

Life is a tremendously exciting, exhilarating, challenging gift, designed to be experienced on all levels. That's why we have five senses. That's why we have a brain and emotions and aspirations and dreams.

Life is for living. Good times and bad. For richer, for poorer. For better, for worse. Commit to life. Love it in all its diversity. It won't last for ever.

For instance, look at the weather, and take it as it comes. Not just the sunny afternoons but the foggy ones too. In the past the diversity of the weather had a radical impact on our daily lives. In these days of central heating and closed environments we cut ourselves off from this elemental magic. There is something glorious about feeling the rain on your face or leaning against the wind while it churns the sea into spray on a blustery day. How long is it since you had a snowball fight or watched the sun rise? Maybe you've never done either of these things? If so, you're missing a treat. Splashing through the puddles on your way to work may not be your idea of heaven but at least the moisture is good for the fat cauliflower you intend to buy for dinner. And think of Gene Kelly singing in the rain. Whatever the weather – love makes it a beautiful day.

Checking out new places, perspectives, climates and civilizations broadens more than our physical horizons. It allows us to savour the sweet distinction of other cultures, unfamiliar mindsets. Getting on a plane or a bus or a train, leaving behind humdrum normality, is a freeing experience in itself.

When I was young I used to say I never wanted to own anything I couldn't pack in a suitcase. Then I got caught up in the materialistic trap. Happily, I am now through that and out the other side. Travel, to places where no one knows you or your history or your reputation, is a great way to prove to yourself that you exist, that you are a valuable human being with or without your mobile phone. It's a lesson in detachment.

When you travel, try to leave behind any preconceived notions of what should be and simply revel in what is. Push back the confines of your comfort zone and be open to change and adventure. Glory in '*la différence*'. With McDonald's practically permeating the furthest reaches of the Orinoco there's little enough that's strange and new these days. Search it out. And when you find it, open yourself to it unreservedly. In the unfamiliarity of new experience you will discover aspects of yourself that you never knew existed. You can shuck off your expected responses and allow yourself the luxury of being as unprogrammed as you were when you were a baby and all the world was new.

The earth's future welfare has been placed in our hands. It is an awesome responsibility but also a tremendous honour. Like the privilege of looking after an ageing parent who has guarded and protected you during your formative years. There's no need to be heavy about it or to turn the whole thing into a colossal chore. Love is about joy. And simple awareness of cause and effect.

Rise each morning in gratitude for the day ahead. Think of how lucky you are to be alive at all. To be healthy and free. To have cornflakes for breakfast. How many people's efforts went into bringing those cornflakes to your table? It's a sobering thought that only a few generations ago you'd not have had the privilege of anything so exotic. You'd have risen in the dark, without benefit of light or hot water, to a bit of bread that you'd had to bake yourself. As for coffee – that was preserved for the rich.

All this largesse is ours before we even consider things like public transport, roads, free schools and libraries, foreign holidays and the ubiquitous TV.

Even if you are living alone on a small income you are still richer than the richest of your ancestors would have been in physical comforts. How would you fancy being sown into your underwear in September to keep you warm in the winter or having to scuttle down to the bottom of the garden to an unheated privy when you wanted to go to the loo?

Make a practice of telling yourself every morning how much you *love* the life you've got. With all its drawbacks, this is a truly wonderful world.

Take time out to review all you've done with your life so far. In your head or on paper, it doesn't matter which. Consider all the things you've accomplished.

Diplomas you've gained. Languages you've learned. Skills you've mastered. Occasions you've enjoyed. Movies and music that have moved you. Lovers you've delighted. Friends you've made. Savour all those good things over again.

Congratulate yourself for your achievements. You and life make a great team.

Muse on all the enjoyable things you're going to do. Revel in the anticipation. Make a list and then *do* them.

Think of all the people you've loved and who have loved you back. Even if they're no longer in your life, they touched a part of it, enriching the moment. Relive the moment. All the moments. That's what the magic of memory is for.

In any obstacle course there are hazards. Face them with courage. And take the best from every negative experience. Make a habit of finding the hidden gold inside the lead balloon. There is always something of value to be gained from every challenging situation. Learn the lesson and rise to the occasion. You are stronger than you know.

So get out there and *love* your life. Be an active participant rather than a passive looker-on. Take chances (not life-threatening chances – be sensible), try new foods, be open to experiment and adventure.

Make the most of it. This is not a rehearsal. When the curtain goes up you are the star. Centre stage. If you muddle about half-heartedly, bump into the furniture, forget your lines or try to upstage your fellow actors, you'll either be booed off or make your final exit to the sound of your own feet. If you pull out all the stops, lay yourself on the line and give the production everything you've got, then be prepared for a standing ovation.

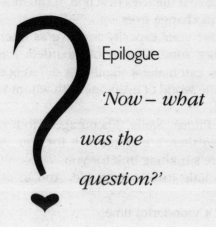

Epilogue

'Now – what was the question?'

So there you are. The answer to life, the universe and everything.

Love.

The fifth element. The final piece in Einstein's last puzzle. If you think of the universe as being manufactured out of love, then the Big Bang was merely an explosion of energy hurling it out to the four corners of infinity. And we are the result. Love made flesh.

Love is everywhere. It permeates everything. How much you experience in your life on a day-to-day basis very much depends on you.

Love is all around waiting to be claimed. It is also inside waiting to be released. Free some up. Like a djinn in an Eastern folktale, once the bottle is decorked, love can only expand and grow . . . into an unstoppable force, an unbeatable ally.

Anything worth doing is improved by an injection of love. Anyone worth knowing is irradiated in its glow. Love is miracles in action. It can move mountains. It can change lives.

Exercise your capacity for love as often as you can. It's not something to be hoarded. Right now, today, you can make a significant difference, for the better, in the world of everyone with whom you come in contact.

Hug. Praise. Smile. Encourage. Motivate. Care. Even when there's nothing in it for you. *Especially* when there's nothing in it for you.

Put a little love in your life. And in everybody else's.

Have a wonderful time.

Love,

Sam.

Useful sources of information

Animal adoption

The Redwing Horse Sanctuary rescues horses, ponies and donkeys from neglect or the knacker's yard and allows them to live out their lives in peace and security. For a small annual fee you can adopt an animal. The Redwing Horse Sanctuary can be contacted at Hill Top Farm, Hall Lane, Frettenham, Norwich NR12 7RW, tel. 01603-737432.

Feng Shui

To find out more about this ancient Eastern philosophy, contact Feng Shui Network International, PO Box 2133, London W1A 1RL, tel. 0171-935 8935.

Genealogy

A good place to start to track down all those lost marriage licences and birth certificates is with an application to the Registrar General of Births, Deaths and Marriages, St Catherine's House, 101 Kingsway, London WC2, tel. 0171-242 0262.

Another good source of advice is The Society of Genealogists, 14 Charterhouse Buildings, London EC2, tel. 0171-251 8799.

For general enquiries and to consult state papers and probate and legal records, contact the Public Record Office, Ruskin Avenue, Kew, Richmond, Surrey TW9 4DU, tel. 0181-876 3444.

Laughter workshops

If you fancy trying one of these, details of courses can be obtained from Robert Holden at the Happiness Project, 185–7 Brompton Road, London SW3 1NE, tel. 0171-581 8838.

Retreats

If you are based in Scotland or the north of England, try the Findhorn Foundation, or the Buddhist enclave on Holy Island. For information on hideaways throughout Britain, contact the National Retreat Centre, Central Hall, 256 Bermondsey Street, London SE1 3UJ, tel. 0171-357 7736.

Self-awareness symposia

One such course is Insight, a seven-day adventure into the self which aims to break down barriers, unplug blockages and give the participant a whole new view of him/herself and the world. Insight is grounded in acceptance and compassion. If you'd like a sneak preview, they do two-hour evening introductory sessions (which are free). The book *You Can't Afford the Luxury of a Negative Thought* (Thorsons) by John-Paul and Peter McWilliams presents many of the ideas behind the programme. Insight can be contacted at 37 Spring Street, London W2 1JA, tel. 0171-706 2021.